From Isa to

Christ

Marvelous McIva,
May you be blessed.
♡ Nona

From Isa to

Christ

A Muslim Woman's Search for the Hand of God

Mona Sabah

GETHSEMANE PRESS

GETHSEMANE PRESS

From Isa to Christ

Copyright © 2017 by Mona Sabah Earnest

This title is also available as an eBook
ISBN-13: 978-0-9986378-0-8 (softcover)

Library of Congress Control Number: [LCCN]: 2017901284
Published by GETHSEMANE PRESS
Edmond, Oklahoma

Scripture taken from the HOLY BIBLE, NEW INTERNATIONAL VERSION ®, Copyright © 1973, 1978, 1984 by International Bible Society, Used by permission of Zondervan. All rights reserved.

Cover Design: Author's Wedding Photo used with Permission
Quran Page Photo (creative commons free photo by firaskaheel 2015:
https://www.flickr.com/photos/firaskaheel/16550852961
Cross Photo (creative commons free photo by cpnyouth.com

Printed in the United States of America

To my faithful and loving husband, Stephen. My testimony cannot be told without your loving support through the years. I am truly grateful that The Lord brought us together in such a beautiful way.

"You are the light of the world. A town built on a hill cannot be hidden. Neither do people light a lamp and put it under a bowl. Instead they put it on its stand, and it gives light to everyone in the house. In the same way, let your light shine before others, that they may see your good deeds and glorify your Father in heaven."

Matthew 5:14-16 (NIV)

May the words of my testimony be pleasing to you, Lord. May they glorify our Lord and Savior Christ Jesus and point only to Him.

Amen.

Contents

Prologue - Hand of God

The fine sand of the desert was something you couldn't get rid of easily. This evening was no different. It was all over his hair, in the folds of his muslin robes, and deep in his nostrils when he breathed. Irritated by the incessant heat and the dirt, he thought about why was he having such a difficult time getting through this throng of people? The dust in his eyes from the hot desert winds along with the sand kicked up from the sandals of the people walking home was making it difficult to see his path. All he knew was that for some reason, he was walking against the flow of the men returning home from work. The sun was setting in front of him, making the sky turn a beautiful deep purple, orange and pink. He knew that darkness quickly approached and evening prayer time was coming up. The crowd could almost feel his own urgency as he began pushing his way through the masses. The streets were not wide open. These Arab towns were built with one home upon another, generations of families living in the same space. The primitive walls of the homes made the alleyways too narrow for the people to go in two directions. He felt like a salmon swimming upstream and he was quickly running out of breath from the exertion.

Just as he thought that the path taken was futile, he felt a rough hand on his elbow. The unseen man grabbed his arm and whisked him into one of the openings draped by a woven blanket that served as a door in the stacked dirt wall. He was rushed through an entryway, which gave way to a paved stone foyer. There was a surprisingly lush garden with a small fountain directly in front of him and a kitchen area to the left. He could hear the clink of pottery and metal as women prepared an evening meal. His eyes had still not adjusted to the darkness of the hallways. The hooded man at his elbow efficiently moved him to the right hand side of the home, which was yet another maze of hallways and rooms. In the Middle East, these types of homes are commonplace. Family homes are added onto by sons and their families generation after generation. Sometimes, the homes can have multiple rooms and living apartments. Several families usually live at their parents' home and are able to commune together.

He tried to clear his crusted eyes with his free hand so he could see his way. His eyes immediately widened and locked on to the light inside the long hallway, as he kept pace with the man who was leading him. He finally dared to ask "Where are you taking me?" and the man at his elbow replied "He has asked specifically for you to come." At that instant, they arrived in a very large room, covered in a mosaic wood paneling with rich furnishings where several men were standing. He did not recognize any of them, including the bearded older man sitting comfortably on the plush hand-knotted rug. While the room spoke of someone of wealth, the man was simply dressed in a white robe of the Arabs. His head was covered with the traditional cloth head piece and his feet were bare. He had a thick leather book with gilt-edged pages open in front of him on a wooden stand that is only reserved for the Holy Quran. He calmly looked up and motioned for him to come and sit down. As he sat down confusedly, the old man opened the book, looked him in the eyes and professed a blessing by raising his right hand, saying "The Hand of God is upon your newborn daughter's head."

With lightening speed, the faceless man who had grabbed him out on the road, abruptly lifted him to standing and in a flash, brought him out into the light outside.

Chapter 1

Destiny

It was Ramadan - the holiest month of the year, on Laylat al Qadr – known in Arabic as the night of destiny or the night of power, the holiest night of Ramadan. This was the night that yet another daughter was born to my parents in the month of November. I was nothing special: a second-born daughter, but still a disgrace, since my father had no sons. My mother happened to be visiting my aunt in Kuwait and I was born during that visit. My parents were living in Taif, Saudi Arabia at the time and I was brought back to our home. My mother was anything but a traditional Muslim woman. She was a medical doctor, an OBGYN who was worth her weight in gold in a Muslim country where women are not able to see a male doctor for their needs without a curtain between them. My father was also a highly educated Telecommunications Engineer who worked at the main television station in the area. I remember slowly driving out to see the towers around the one, lonely television broadcasting outpost that he managed in the Taif.

I grew up in Saudi Arabia and learned to speak Arabic. I watched Sesame Street and the Muppets in Arabic whenever they aired on the television. In fact, I did not know that they did not speak Arabic all the time until I saw them in the United States! Of course, there was no Miss Piggy – pigs are considered unclean, even in a puppet form. At home, my parents spoke English to me and my older sister so that we would have a grasp on what they considered to be the "universal language." When I turned five, I was flown to Islamabad, Pakistan (my parent's country) to attend school and learn Urdu, my own language and customs. I went with my nanny, Abbai and the flight there was traumatic for me. I had never been separated from my parents before and was flying to an unknown life without them. I have early memories of laying on the cold hallway floor of my all-girls school in Pakistan, crying and refusing to go to class. My poor nanny ended up attending a few months of Kindergarten with me. I specifically remember her glaring at me as she perched upon a tiny chair while I colored the letter "I" for Iron. It did not bother me that I was making her go to school with me. She was there for me only (well, she was there for my sister also, but I reasoned that my sister was five years older and did not need her as much as I did). On the days I was inconsolable, the school teachers would allow me to sit underneath my sister's school desk but my sister would often kick me out of frustration because no ten year old wants a crying baby sitting at her feet. A better solution was found when I was allowed to be in my own classroom, with my Abbai to watch over me as I played and colored.

After a few months, I was better acclimated to my routine without my parents and with that comfort, my real personality traits emerged. The five year old little girl who loved to talk too much in grade school class still loves to talk. I was not the most well-behaved child. I was obedient but to a point. When the teacher would turn her back, I would talk some more or pass notes. I can remember vividly having to stand outside the hallway for punishment, running through the Principal's prized rose garden while ignoring the thorns that tore my freshly pressed uniform, being made to sit in her office for detention, and my refusing to do anything during the Physical Education class. Maybe that's why exercise is still abhorrent to me.

The Principal took pity on me and gradually began to invite me into her office, especially on the evenings when no one from my family remembered to pick me up from school. I used to cry outside in the school yard and become frightened, but she would put her arms around my shoulders and gently lead me to her office, where I would play quietly until someone came to get me. This was the way it was for me until my parents came back to Pakistan from Saudi Arabia.

My mother was expecting another child and wanted this one to be born in her country, so my parents decided to move back. This was during the time when husbands waited outside the delivery room in the hospital, especially in a third world Muslim country. I remember waiting outside with my father for news of the baby, when my aunt came running out of the room into the long hallway, crying uncontrollably. I looked up and saw my father's face go pale. He asked her "is there something wrong with my wife?" She shook her head. "Did something go wrong with the delivery?" She shook her head again. She then said "Brother, I don't want to tell you this, but you have the shame of another daughter." My dad was very upset – not about having another girl, but about the way my aunt thought about his girls. I was proud of him when he told her that "don't you know that every child is a blessing from Allah?" and he went inside to see his beloved wife and new daughter.

In the following years, we moved around from country to country, for my father to pursue better job opportunities. We lived for a short time in London, England, spent a few months in Abu Dhabi, United Arab Emirates and then my parents finally decided to sell everything in Pakistan and move permanently to the United States. My father received two job opportunities as an Engineer: one offer was in Virginia and the other was in California. When we first arrived in New York City in 1981, we experienced a true culture shock. In my mere ten years of life, I had never seen anything quite like it – not even in our brief time in England. Things were so fast paced and so different than our life in Pakistan. My dad notified the new company in California that he would prefer to stay on the East

Coast, since my mother's brother lived there, but the organization said that there would be a bonus offered if he could start in a week.

We bought a two-toned Buick Skylark, packed our six suitcases that we brought with us from Pakistan and drove across the United States in three days. My dad did not realize how vast this country is – it was no problem to drive across Pakistan, which is approximately the size of California. His job offered a furnished apartment in the Bay Area, but my parents had some friends who lived in Stockton, located in California's fertile Central Valley.

By this time, the family was wondering when we would finally settle down and move out of our suitcases. Stockton was a good solution for my parents. In fact, they ended up moving right next door to friends we had in Islamabad. They were not only friends, but distant relatives who provided safety and security in a new land. They helped introduce my family to the tight-knit Muslim community. This community was mostly Pakistanis, but also included a few families from Africa.

Our family was able to put down some roots and stay close to our culture. The closest mosque was in a farming town called Lodi, which was a short drive from our home. I remember going to the non-descript mosque for major holidays and weddings. Other than that, my dad went whenever conscience prompted him to do so – usually on a Friday, so he could check in with his Muslim friends and meet with the men in the community. Those infrequent visits to the mosque did not do much for our faith, but they did help to establish our place in the Muslim society.

I entered school in the middle of the fifth grade and found the adjustment exceedingly difficult. The other children knew that I was different and I was teased for smelling like curry (which I am sure I did). Also, I didn't dress the same, talk the same or have the same interests in things as them. Even though we lived in a Muslim community, my parents did not make their daughters cover their hair and we were allowed to wear American clothes except for shorts, short skirts or tank tops (a rule of modesty I now apply to our daughter). My mother told me that was the main reason to leave Pakistan – there was a possibility that a law would be passed that would require girls ten and older to cover themselves with a burqa veil for school. Since that would seriously impede learning, she was completely opposed to anything that stood in the way of education for her daughters. In Pakistan, rules for covering and clothing are a bit more relaxed than other Muslim countries. They allow a shawl (called a dupata in Urdu) to function as a head cover and the more fashionable young ladies simply throw it over their shoulders. In addition, we were allowed to wear outfits with short sleeves in Pakistan – something never done in the Arabian countries in which we had lived.

My older sister had an even sharper learning curve since she immediately entered right into high school, which can be a brutal place for any teenager. We were fresh-off-the-plane immigrants who did not understand the need for deodorant (she helped us all learn quickly) and the absolute high school requirement for the 1980's – a curling iron. With my older sister's helpful flexibility and keen sense of style, we were able to adjust to the cultural differences and settle into a new routine at school. At this time, my indefatigable mother was studying to take her Foreign Medical Graduate Exams (which she passed immediately) and then went back to Medical School for a post-graduate specialization degree in Psychiatry. A brilliant mother with a degree in psychiatry had a decidedly unfair advantage over her daughters in knowing how to interrogate us and knowing what we were up to. In high school, I was allowed to join scholastic clubs and run for office in student government. In fact, I relished the fact that I was the class president for my freshman and junior years. My parents encouraged their daughters to excel in their studies, but we were not allowed to pursue extraneous things such as art, drama, or music. We were not allowed to date, since there was no need for that with arranged marriages for each one of us. After a few years of freedom in the United States, I thought that was just a threat even though I had been told that I would have an arranged marriage since I was a little girl and it was deemed so by tradition.

When the Senior prom came, I helped with the set up and the selling of tickets, though I knew I would not be allowed to go. I had gone to a dance before, but I was only allowed to go with a group of friends as long as there were no boyfriends. I knew that the prom would be a different story – no one went as a group at that time. About two weeks before the prom, I was lamenting to my friends that I wished I could have this as a memory of my high school years. They told me to ask my parents – maybe they would have changed their minds? Since my parents were immigrants, I thought that I could probably use that to my advantage. So, I decided upon a little white lie… I told them that the prom was a requirement for high school graduation. They said "by all means, you have to go! But you have to go with a group." I was elated… then was quickly devastated. With two weeks to go, who would I go with? All the "good" dates were taken by this time.

I was having lunch with some friends and one of them had a photo album of a recent trip to Santa Cruz. There was a very good looking young man in the photos and I asked this friend if he was dating anyone. He looked at me and said "he is not your type." I told him that it didn't matter what type of a guy it was, as long as I had a good looking date for the prom. This was not supposed to be an ever-lasting relationship – just a date for that singular opportunity I would have to experience American culture at its fullest. After a lot of cajoling, he told me that he would ask his friend if he wanted to go on a blind date for the prom (but that it was highly unlikely this would happen, as the guy in question had graduated high school the year before). My friend Jeff said that it would be a lot easier to convince him (Stephen) if he had at least met me in passing, so we set up this elaborate scheme, where Jeff stopped by Stephen's home and had me there, in tow.

That evening, Jeff called him and said he knew a "nice" girl who needed a date to the prom and would he double date with them? The first thing Stephen said was "No." Then he asked "What's wrong with her? Why can't she find her own date for the prom?" Instead of a long, drawn-out explanation, Jeff simply replied "She's Muslim." Stephen asked "Then why is she able to go to the prom? I thought Muslims couldn't date?" Jeff said "She lied to her parents." He felt sorry for me and told Jeff that if there was a tuxedo left in his size (it was one week before the prom now), that he would go, but he first wanted to get to know me better. Jeff knew I was not allowed to date, so he said that would be a challenge. He gave me his number so I could call him. When we talked, he told me that he would go with me to the prom, but that he needed to find a tuxedo. Since we had one formal wear shop in our area of town, it would be a tough thing to do last minute. He called me the next day – they had one tuxedo left in his size.

We had a wonderful time at the dance and I knew that I would probably have to burn the pictures of us, since that kind of evidence would never be acceptable to my parents or to my future husband. We decided to see each other in groups and I knew that I was going to attend the University of Southern California (USC), so our time together was short-lived. At the end of the summer, as I was planning to go to Southern California, my parents decided that it would be too far from home and they would rather that I attend a local university and stay close to their home. They enrolled me in a small private university in Stockton. I was furious.

In our culture, parents have absolute authority and control over their children's lives. They determine our career, our marriage, our education. Everything. It is simply a given and you don't question it. Islam means to submit and a part of being a Muslim child is being taught submission to parents, to the community (the Ummah) and to God. There was nothing I could do about this decision. Furthermore, my parents informed me that they had enrolled me in the School of Dentistry so I could become a dentist (I was scared to death of dentists and had been known to pass out in the dental chair from time to time – still do). Whatever the cost, I was to obey my parents in this, so I attended this college.

The good news was that I was still in the same town, so I gave Stephen a call to let him know that I was still around. He seemed happy to hear that and even came by my dorm room (it was a requirement for Freshmen to live in the dormitory their first year) to see me and meet my roommate. We saw each other a lot that year and began to date secretly. He knew that my parents would not approve of that and he also knew that I was slated to eventually have an arranged marriage. Since I lived away from my parents (they had since moved back to the Bay Area for my father's job – he had been commuting all along for many years), I was relatively free. I was required to come home every weekend and to call them every night to check in with them. If they called and I did not answer, well, then there was a price to pay for that. There was little to no trust and it made my parents nervous to have one of their daughters out of their reach and ensconced in a different community.

After a year of this, my parents told me that it was time to move home. They did not like me to even be an hour and a half away and that they wanted me to be back where I could help out the family and they could keep an eye on me. I moved back home and went to a community college nearby. He still came to see me when I was in class and he would drive all that way just to take me out to lunch.

After tasting so much freedom, I started to feel suffocated in my parents' home. My lucky break came when I was granted admission to the University of California, Davis. I convinced my parents that it would be beneficial for me to go there so I could study pre-med and go to medical school… just like my mother. This was a good plan, as I preferred medicine more than dentistry and was serious about my studies. Of course, the biggest plus was being closer to the one I loved.

I moved to Davis (which was about an hour and a half away in another direction) and around the same time, he was admitted to California State University, Sacramento. This meant that we would be only forty minutes away from each other and could continue to date. The close proximity allowed us to get to know each other better. In my senior year in college, he asked me if I was seriously considering him or if I was seriously considering an arranged marriage. I told him that it was not mine to consider - an arranged marriage was destined for me and I could not do anything about it.

My older sister had just graduated from Pharmacy School and

within two weeks of her graduation, she and my mother flew to Pakistan to arrange her marriage. This snapped me out of my little daydream world. I was shocked. I was shocked that my parents were actually going to go through with it. I knew of some Muslim couples who had met here in the States and got to know each other so that it would not be a complete arranged marriage and was hoping I could fit into that category – maybe they would choose someone here that I knew. She was given two choices: this guy or that one. Since she did not know either man and had just met them on that trip, she chose one relatively blindly. The next thing I knew, they had a betrothal, a wedding date and had printed announcements of their upcoming marriage mailed out.

His family arrived from Pakistan with great fanfare. My mother spent weeks getting the house and all of us ready for this event. I was given marching orders on how to behave when they came to our home. I was told by my mother that I was to act as demurely as possible, not look at the men in the eye, say salaam to the parents, not say anything extra and then leave to go fetch tea for everyone. I waited to be called down to be introduced. My mother was very cheerful and said "This is Mona, our middle daughter." Without even looking up, the fiancée snapped his fingers at me and said "Hey! Water!" I defiantly raised my head and I glared at my mother. Then, I looked at him and snapped my fingers and said "Hey! It's in the faucet!" My mother grabbed me by my ear and yanked me out of the room. I heard her go back and apologize to everyone, saying that her other daughters were not like "that one."

My sister's fiancée was a piece of work. He thought that the world revolved around him and for the most part, in Pakistan, it did! The oldest sons are the ones with the inheritance. They are the chosen ones and they get to partake in the best things in the family. He was doted on by his mother and expected everyone to treat him that way as well. I was told that he was from the chosen line of the Prophet Muhammad's family – he was from the house of Hussein and was a Sayed. To me, it did not mean a thing but to my parents, it was a sign from Allah as a blessing on the entire family.

Her wedding was a long, drawn-out affair. In our culture, Pakistan is very closely aligned with India and their customs. It should be noted that Pakistan gained independence from India in 1947, so there are still strong ties to the cultural customs, but not to the Hindu religion. The religion was the cause of the civil war between India and Pakistan. There were days of celebration and one of my favorite celebrations is "Mehndi." Mehndi is the name for a paste made out of henna leaves and it is used for drawing intricate decorations on the hands and feet of the bride and women in the wedding party. The ritual signals the start of the wedding preparations for the bride and is meant to beautify her for her husband. The ceremony usually takes place in the bride's parents' home, where the groom's family brings the Mehndi in large trays that are adorned with votive candles, flowers, sweets, money, fruit, nuts, and dates. Some Muslims believe that dyeing their hair or beards with henna is in line with a hadith (tradition) of Mohammad. There is also a commonly held belief that he told women to wear henna on their hands so they can beautify themselves and in this way, be different than a man.

Since my sister's future in-laws were not from the United States, they flew in for the ceremonies. In addition, many of her friends took the place of his family, in bringing the large Mehndi platters to our home. The festivities began with grand celebration. My parents had hired Pakistani musicians who played at our home and also guests had flown in from various countries for the occasion. The groom's party came in at the appointed time in the evening.

However, the groom did not show up with them. My parents were very confused by this, as this is an important custom – to usher in the groom with the party that brings the Mehndi. In fact, when he failed to appear for several hours after the time he was supposed to, my sister, the bride began to cry. A crying daughter makes any father angry and my dad was no exception. He came to me, as I sat by her in the middle of the party and bade me to come with him to another room. He let his anger get the best of him upstairs in my parents' bedroom and as he vented, probably told me more than what I needed to know about this situation. He had said that the family was being very disrespectful and the groom especially so by not arriving on time. Lateness is common and customary for most Pakistanis but not several hours late. To hinder marriage festivities was unheard of, unless the family had decided to call off the marriage. He was greatly upset that the latter might be true and that his beloved daughter was going to be dishonored in front of all his guests. I offered simple encouragement by telling him to call the family, in case there was an accident or something terrible had occurred. My dad would not do that. He said that if they did not come in the next hour, the marriage was off. It was a matter of preserving his honor and doing the right thing for his daughter.

As we were talking upstairs, there was a large commotion downstairs. The bridegroom had finally arrived – with no mention whatsoever of why he was over four hours late. This was not a very fortuitous beginning to a marriage that was literally between families. My sister, however, was relieved and the celebration continued with songs and dancing into the evening.

The wedding reception was also a very lavish affair. Several days after the Mehndi, they were married by an Imam (leader of the mosque) with just the parents present. In fact, I didn't even know the official wedding ceremony was taking place. There was a grand reception after the ceremony and there was more food, dancing, flowers, guests I had never met, and of course, lots of sweets.

I was in college at the time of her wedding and was still unsure about my own future. I paid close attention to what was happening with my sister and thought that since my parents were in favor of her marriage, she was set for success in her future. She ended up marrying a Pakistani doctor and seemed to be relatively happy about her marriage. My parents were in full support, even with the huge slight shown by his family during the Mehndi ceremony.

I had been secretly dating Stephen for almost two years at this time. He lived about an hour and a half away, so we could not see each other with much frequency during this time. It was a very difficult time for me, especially, as I was being torn between culture, duty and what I felt to be love. I believed that the year apart would show if it was merely an infatuation or a more permanent relationship.

Since I was away at school, the ability to have some freedom from my parents' home and to have Stephen so close by was heady. We were both studying Science as our major, so our school schedule was demanding. Yet, we both found time to be with each other and share what we were doing. I was still required to commute home each weekend and that added to the stress of my studies. My parents were not sure I was applying myself as much as I could (I was taking a full load of 18 credits per semester, plus full time summer school each year) and they wanted me to graduate in three years instead of four. The pressure and stress of a science curriculum combined with my parents' demands was almost too much for me to bear. I still have nightmares about missing a class or forgetting a final exam.

He was my outlet. He was able to help me to overcome my fears of failure and he helped to stabilize my thinking but I was not sure how long he was going to stick around. I was feeling a lot of pressure from my parents about being married according to their will. I knew that in order to thwart their plans, I would have to continue on to graduate school. For if I was in school, my parents promised me that I would not be rushed into marriage. An eternity in school was sounding pretty good right about then, since I dreaded who they would choose for me. They had hinted at some plans to marry me to a family in England or possibly one in Pakistan. I didn't even want to think or talk to them about either scenario.

It was around this time that he asked me to marry him. It wasn't the most romantic proposal, or even a formal one. Even though there were no bells or whistles or surprises, I still remember that day at his parent's home. We went to say hello to them and were sitting in their living room. He took my hand and looked into my eyes. He said "What do you think about your sister's marriage?" I looked at him with disdain in my eyes - he already knew that answer. Then he said "How in the world will you make it through an arranged marriage with a Muslim man? I know you and your personality. You haven't been raised as a typical Muslim woman, who has been taught to be submissive to men. In fact, your parents have given you much freedom and liberty by bringing you here to the United States and educating you. I really think that if you have an arranged marriage, you will never make it. A Muslim man is never going to abide by your views - especially one straight from Pakistan." Then he said, "Why don't you marry me instead? I know you and love you." I told him that I loved him also, but reminded him that my relationship with my parents was the biggest obstacle to my being able to marry him. He was very wise in his assessment of the situation and told me that he understood clearly that if I chose to marry him, it would disrupt or even destroy everything I currently knew: my relationship with parents, family, extended family, culture, religion, and any children we had in the future. He blatantly said that if I chose him, it may very well mean that I would be disowned by my parents and that our children would not know or have grandparents on my side of the family.

For a young college girl, that was a very difficult choice. I did not take it lightly. My world and existence revolved around my parents. They were never mean or cruel to me. In fact, they sacrificed and worked hard to provide me every luxury, including paying for my college, my car, clothes, everything. To leave all that behind and take on an unknown future? Could I actually do that for this person?

I thought it through and we decided to be married in August after I graduated from college. We would print out the wedding invitations and hand one to my parents. Talk about being immature and not facing the situation in the right manner! When the invitations had been printed, I drove home after classes one evening and walked into my parents' bedroom. By the grace of God, my father was not there as I handed the invitation to my mom who absolutely exploded.

I tell people that the scene was just like one of those Bruce Willis action thrillers... I was running out of the room and their home in slow motion, while the building was exploding all around me. It was not brave, it was just a scared twenty year old who chose a cowardly way to deliver life changing news to her mother and father.

I think about that situation today. Even as an American, that type of a situation would not have ended well... why in the world did I think it was going to be okay with my parents? I believe the best way to explain the action is to say that I believed with all my heart that my parents would ship me off on the next plane to Pakistan (especially given threats in the past from my father, including showing me an airline ticket to Pakistan and telling me that my name would be on it if I stepped out of line) to get me married immediately if I hesitated at all in my decision. Printing that decision off on white embossed paper seemed to be the right thing to do at that time.

When I got back to my college apartment with my roommates, there was complete silence. The girls looked at me in anticipation and fear as I silently stared back at them and then ran into my room to burst into tears. Stephen came over to find out how it went but from my heartbroken sobs, he already knew.

The next evening, I received a call from my parents' home. It was my older sister who was acting as the spokesperson for the family. She told me that my father said I would burn in hell for this action. In one action, I had gone against our culture, hundreds of years of traditions, our religion, our community, our family, and his place at the head of our family. He had disowned me as a daughter and I had shamed him and brought the highest dishonor to them. No one in the family would come or be allowed to come to this wedding. It was over.

Until that phone call, I was still clinging to a little girl dream that love would make everything alright. That my parents wouldn't possibly do something like that to me - I was a beloved child! It broke my heart and I know that decision broke my parents' hearts as well. Instead of a wedding, a funeral was taking place on both sides of the phone. There was bitter mourning for I was dead to them.

Chapter 2

Disowned

Help came from the strangest and least expected place. My maternal grandfather, whom we lovingly called "Abba," lived with my parents. He was completely devoted to Islam in his later life prayed five times a day and read the Quran nightly. Before I ran out of my parents' home after I detonated the "I'm getting married, hope you can make it" bomb, I did have the wherewithal to kiss my Abba and tell him briefly what had happened. Being a quiet man with a quiet demeanor, he didn't really say anything. He just gave me a kiss back and told me goodbye. Apparently, my Abba was the one who sat down with my parents and told them that he knew what was going on. He asked both of them to listen to reason - time on this earth was fleeting. Did they really want to throw away a relationship with their daughter without even hearing her side of the story? Did they not realize that they were the ones who brought her here to the United States to give her freedom that she would never have had in Pakistan or in the Middle East? Did they not realize that they were the progressive, educated parents who had raised an equally progressive, educated and head-strong mule of a daughter?

I received a phone call almost two months later from my mom. She was very tentative in her approach, but asked me if I was going to be a Christian now. This question seemed to come out of nowhere and I was so confused. Stephen was a Christian in name only, but of course my parents did not know that. He did not go to church. He had gone before in the past when he was younger, but it was hit and miss. For me to be a Christian would mean that I would turn my back on God. That thought wasn't even on my mind. It would be inconceivable for me to turn my back on what I knew as a child and the culture I loved. I was truly embedded in my identity as a Muslim.

When I reacted in confusion about why my mother would think this as an automatic outcome of my marriage, she plainly stated that in Islam, a woman cannot even marry a Christian man (Quran 2:221) and there were special rules surrounding Muslim men marrying Christian or Jewish women (only these two are allowed, but they would convert to his religion - Quran 60:10).

Another factor behind my mother's question stems from the fact that if you are born in a Muslim country, you are automatically a Muslim. No questions asked, no other options given. It is safe and permissible for anyone to assume that one hundred percent of people born in Saudi Arabia are Muslim. There is no other choice given to them. A Christian Arab was something I had never considered until I met one after I accepted Christ!

Conversely, many Muslims believe that if you are born in a "Christian" country such as the United States, you are automatically a Christian. I was also under that assumption. My frame of reference only dealt with absolutes. Atheism was not ever considered a possibility. That was just ridiculous to a Muslim mind! With this assumption, my parents concluded (as I did) that he and his family were fully committed Christians.

I told my mom that I had no intentions of changing my religion, as we were in the 20th Century and not in 600 AD. She was very surprised to hear that I would want a proper Muslim wedding and that he would agree to this as well. We had decided that we would be married at a church and were already talking to a kind pastor who agreed to marry us if we did our homework. We met with him on several occasions, so I did not think it was out of the question if we were to be married by an Imam (Muslim leader and holy person) as well.

At this news, my mother asked if his mother would want to meet with them. The occasion was arranged but my father did not attend. My mom warmly welcomed Stephen's mother and met him for the first time at our family home. It was agreed that the wedding would be postponed a few months from August to January so they could arrange for the Imam and also announce the news to their friends and community.

My father met him for the very first time at our rehearsal dinner on a Thursday evening. Poor Stephen had lost about ten to fifteen pounds from the sheer stress of this process. We had a small wedding party gathering and all our family got to meet one another for the first time... the day before our wedding.

The Muslim wedding is so very different than a Christian one. I thought I had attended many weddings over my childhood, but soon realized that I had never attended a Nikah. My sister had gone to Pakistan with only my mother when her Nikah had occurred. A Nikah is essentially a marriage contract between two families. The father is the guardian and in some cultures, consent is also required of the grandfather[1]. Only the immediate male members of the family are allowed to be present and the Imam who conducts the wedding process.

I was dressed in a beautiful cream colored silk Pakistani shalwar kameez suit that had a matching hand-embroidered dupata veil or head covering. I went to the ceremony and was shown to a separate room where I was joined by my two sisters, mother, his mother and his paternal grandmother. The Imam showed the groom to a side room to join his father, paternal

---

[1] The Encyclopedia of Islam, New Edition, Vol. VIII, p. 27, Leiden 1995

grandfather, my father and my Abba. All the men congregated on one side and all the women on another. There was much talk and general conversation that was going on in the women's side. In fact, I began to wonder after some time why no one was coming to get me. After what seemed to be an eternity, my father came in to congratulate Stephen's mother. I saw him standing behind the men. He was straight-faced, pale and looked like he was about to throw up.

There was a large ledger-type of a book where I was to sign my name and after I did that, my father paid the Imam for performing the ceremony. The Imam didn't bother looking at me. He only spoke to me once the entire time. I only saw a glimpse of him as he was walking to the other room and then I saw him when I signed the book. There was no formal contract or any type of a paper that showed we were married.

In Islamic marriages, the woman does not play an active role. Her father or grandfather does the negotiations (if any) and offers her hand in marriage. There is a consent, but if a family forces the woman, one would not know due to the shame culture. It would be dishonorable for a woman to get to the altar and then say no to a wedding most likely arranged by her family. There would be consequences for a decision like that. Of course in my case, my parents knew that I wanted this marriage more than anything. I was alright with no one asking me anything. It did make me nervous to think afterwards that I did not even see my beloved go into the room - I could have married anyone!

It's interesting to me that my Western friends do not understand the passage from Genesis where Jacob "accidentally" marries Leah instead of his first love, Rachel. After having lived through an Eastern wedding ceremony where both sides do not establish a marriage contract in front of one another, this possibility becomes more understandable. I was far more understanding of what happened to Jacob in the Bible. If there was a ceremony like ours where there was a divider in between and the woman (Leah or Rachel in this case) were not even asked whether or not they wished to marry the unseen man on the other side of the room - who would have realized what was happening? After the ceremony takes place and the men shake hands... it's all too late. Fortunately for me, it truly was Stephen on the other side and we were now officially married according to Islam and as the Quran dictates.

That evening, we had a Mehndi celebration. There was celebration dancing for the family and guests. Sadly not for me, for the bride has no fun and just sits there, looking demurely down at her feet. As discussed in the earlier chapter, the Mehndi celebration is not necessarily a Muslim tradition, but is more aligned with Pakistan's Indian roots. Mehndi is used to celebrate Eid (after Ramadan) and also weddings. It is a burst of vivid color, as the bride wears traditional colors of yellow or green and is a time of great enjoyment for the guests, who are similarly adorned in bright colored clothes. The bride and the groom are allowed to attend together, but the groom sits at a distance away from the bride. Stephen sat in a chair apart from me as the women in the family crowded around to apply henna paste to decorate my hands and feet.

The next morning, on Saturday, we had our church ceremony and were married in a small chapel at the Fremont Presbyterian Church in Sacramento by Pastor Dexter McNamara. My parents came late, which caused me great distress because of all that had happened so far. I panicked and almost started crying because I thought that they backed out. But they did not let me down. We were not sure my father was going to walk me down the aisle but he did so, in his love for me. At the last minute, my dad actually condescended and agreed to do that for me on my wedding day.

I was exhilarated... I got to marry the man I loved and my parents were there. God was truly amazing.

Saturday evening we had a wedding reception. This was an East meets West gathering where I came in my white church dress, cut the cake, had a hasty first dance, and then was whisked away to change into a proper Pakistani wedding dress. This dress was the most beautiful thing I had seen, and even more special because my dad helped choose it. It was a long red silk kurta shirt with deep green pajamas, a long vest with red and green silk and gold embroidery, all topped with a heavy hand-embroidered dupata veil that weighed almost fifteen pounds. It was so heavy, it kept falling off my head. My parents were very gracious in arranging the reception. They invited over three hundred friends, but only about a tenth of them came.

[Left] Wedding Veil slipping   [Right] Wedding Banquet

We were all exhausted from the events of the previous days, combined with the stress of meeting family for the first time. So when someone pulled the fire alarm during the reception, it was almost a sigh of relief on both of our part. It was starting to rain outside and our entire wedding party had to walk out. There was no fire... only fire trucks that made it easy for wedding guests to leave abruptly. When the "all clear" was given, there were only the closest friends and family left. My father gave me my own copy of the Quran and my mother had sewn a red satin cover with a tassel tie for it. Many Muslims place a decorative cover on their Holy Book. He held the Quran over my head as I stepped into the car to leave reminding me of the blessing that God watches over us.

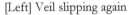
[Left] Veil slipping again   [Right] Walking out under the Quran

We had a short drive to our honeymoon in Reno and it was hard to believe the ordeal of the ceremony was over. It was hard to believe we were now able now to spend the rest of our lives together as husband and wife. To walk into our own apartment in peace and quiet and no agonizing turmoil was a luxury and a blessing.

A few days after we came back from our honeymoon, my mother called me in tears and told me to not do something rash. Again, I had no idea what she was talking about. She said that several Muslim women had called her and told her that the only reason I wanted to marry because I was pregnant. I told my mother very calmly there was no possibility that was true and she only had to wait a few months to find out the truth! I also reminded her that she had done her job in raising me as a good Muslim girl. The women were only trying to stir up rumors in an attempt to explain to their own families and community as the only reason a Muslim girl would want to marry a Christian boy.

Wedded bliss was evident in our little home and we started to open the wedding gifts. So many of the Muslim families brought elaborately wrapped packages - thick beautiful paper, huge bows, silk flowers with all the trimmings. You could tell that they had gone together to have the gifts wrapped - they looked similar. As we began to open the gifts, Stephen noticed that one of the packages was a bit damp on a corner. Although it had been several days since the wedding, we didn't think much about this, as our wedding reception had ended with rain. We opened up a gorgeously wrapped gift package and found it had a completely broken glass vase. It was a disappointment that the vase may have fallen apart in moving the packages from the reception to our apartment. The next package from a Pakistani family had a broken frame with a cracked glass, along with crumpled newspapers and other papers. One of the largest and most elaborately wrapped package contained empty soup cans, banana peels along with other miscellaneous garbage. This was the package that had been leaking onto the other gifts of trash given to us.

My eyes welled up and I broke down in tears. I knew exactly what these gifts meant: We will come to your wedding for the "show," but we will NEVER accept this in our homes. Later as a Christian, I came across Jesus Christ's words " Woe to you, teachers of the law and Pharisees, you hypocrites! You are like whitewashed tombs, which look beautiful on the outside but on the inside are full of the bones of the dead and everything unclean" (Matthew 23:27). They came wearing beautiful smiles and embroidered dresses, carrying lovely gifts that were painstakingly wrapped for their beauty. Inside the trappings contained the true sentiments of their hearts - refuse, garbage and broken glass, intended to harm, destroy and send a very clear message -- we will never accept this marriage within our community.

My childish reaction was to run to mommy and daddy to tell them what happened. My sweet and discerning husband told me to not share this with my family. They had done all they could to present a true face to the Muslim community that said their daughter was entering into an honorable marriage in a Muslim way.

They did the right thing for us. It was not their burden to bear. The community will not go against the Quran which states that Muslim women do not have the choice to marry outside their faith. They did not want their daughters to witness this as acceptable behavior and we would never be welcomed to their home or into their community.

After a few months of being married, my mother asked me which families had invited us to their home. It is tradition that the married couple go to each family's home and be greeted accordingly. None of that happened. I just told my mom that we had been too busy with graduation and with starting my new job. I could not bear to tell her the truth of their community's message. I knew that my parents had tried to follow tradition as best as they could for me, by allowing me to be married by an Imam and also to invite the Muslim community so that they would see that my intent was to stay a Muslim. It was a painful lesson for me to learn about what the community believed and how they conveyed a very clear and painful message to me and my husband about the way they felt about this marriage.

The Muslim community ("Ummah" in Arabic) has a dual meaning. It not only means the Muslim community in which one lives, but also the collective Muslim community all over the world. The community dictates right and wrong according to the Quran and the community can also decide what to participate in and who to admonish. The community spread the rumors about my wedding because no one could believe that someone would actually marry outside the Ummah. They also showed their true colors and intentions in the gifts they brought.

Despite their actions, God truly did have His hand on us. My mother's concern about the pregnancy rumor dissipated, since we waited almost four years to have a baby. By that time, my mom was getting impatient for a grandchild from us. It became a time of sweet anticipation.

Chapter 3

What's in a Name?

I am asked about my name by many people, especially when they find out I am Pakistani. Usually, they ask "Is 'Mona' a common name in Pakistan?" The answer is no, it's not a common name at all. In Kuwait, the Al-Sabah Sheikhs are the only ones allowed to hold ruling positions. Out of homage and deference to the ruling family, I was given the name "Sabah" when I was born. My parents also considered the fact that in Arabic, it means bright, or morning. This was a complete misnomer for me, as I am a night owl and have been since I was little. It's easier for me to stay up late into the night than to get up early. My nickname was Mona. This was given to me by my father's brother who passed away when he was young. I never had the chance to know my uncle, but after his death, everyone called me this name in his remembrance. The meaning of the name Mona is a bit more difficult to find. In Arabic, it means wish or desire. I am not sure if any of those would be applicable to me.

Names have always been interesting to me. In the eastern cultures, the family's name as well as the individual's name is given great thought. In Muslim cultures, one can tell a lot about a person from their name. For example, "Abdallah" means Abd - servant of, plus Allah - God. Muhammad or Mohammad (either spelling accepted) is a very common prefix to a family name. Many times, names also include their family or clan. We had decided on the name of our first child even before we had children. We both liked the name Jacob for a boy. I wanted a name that would translate well to my language (Yaqub) and Stephen thought it was a strong name. I did not know that Jacob meant "supplanter" or even "deceiver." In the Bible, Jacob ends up being one who struggles with God and then gets a great blessing to become Israel.

Paying attention to my family's origins, we chose my maiden name as our oldest son's middle name. For a contingency plan, we agreed on Sarah for a baby girl. My best friend in Kindergarten in Pakistan was Sarah and his great grandmother was Sarah Dalton.

In Pakistan and also for many Eastern cultures it is believed that a person's name has a lot to do with what kind of characteristics they will have when they grow up. There is significance associated not only with the first name, but also the middle name. So we decided that since Jacob was found both in the Quran and the Bible, that meant the name was blessed by God. That would make for a good name for an eldest son. I did not realize that the name Sarah was in the Bible, as many girls in Pakistan had that name in different variations. I just thought it would be a pretty name. We looked up the meaning for Sarah and found that it meant "princess." It is interesting to note that while Abraham is highly regarded in Islam, Sarah (Abraham's wife) is not mentioned by name in the Quran. She is only mentioned in the Hadith and is called "Abraham's wife."

From the Bible, we see that names matter to God. He gives people new names and in other places he changes them. Psalm 147:4 even goes as far as to say "He determines the number of the stars and calls them each by name." Also, there are many names in the Quran that coincide with the Bible. Muslims believe that if you choose a name from the Quran for your child, they will receive a special blessing from God.

Our firstborn was Jacob. He was a very difficult birth and ended up being in step down NICU for five days after he was born. He had left shoulder dystocia due to use of forceps and did not breathe for several minutes after delivery. He was a whopping 8 pounds 14 ounces. For a mom who is barely 5'1" it was a difficult delivery! Right after he was delivered, the nurse placed him upon my chest and announced "It's a boy!" The entire room stood silent, as the baby was silent. The same nurse then screamed "He's not breathing!" A flurry of activities took place off to the side and an emergency code was called by the nurses. After that, I blacked out from fear and loss of blood.

When I awoke in the post partum room, no one told me if my

baby had lived or died. My husband and mother were nowhere to be found. I asked the attending nurse about my baby and she told me that I had lost a lot of blood and to rest. She was sure that the hospital staff was taking care of the baby. I was in hysterics. Again, I blacked out - most likely from fear. When I woke up, it was morning and I still did not know if the baby was alive. I knew that the only one who would help me was God. I said a prayer to Him even though I was bleeding from childbirth (bleeding women are not allowed to approach God in prayer in Islam. It is expressly forbidden). I knew that God would hear my prayers for my baby.

My husband arrived and told me that he could take me up to the NICU to see our child. I cried so many tears because this was the first time someone told me that he was alive. The Intensive Care Pediatrician spoke to us about a long list of things that could be wrong with him. They said he may have permanent brain damage and that he may not be fully able to use his shoulder. The entire time he was speaking to me, I knew that God would heal this child and that there would be nothing wrong with him. There was no question in my mind that even if something happened to this boy, that God would make him better. I did not know that The Lord was slowly building my faith in Him. The staff was amazed to see Jacob's quick recovery. I knew in my heart there was nothing wrong with him. God provided a son for us and God would see him through. It was as simple as that.

What's in a Name?

Our next child came with less drama and trauma. We insisted that the new doctor look at the previous delivery records and plan a C-section. Joshua was born to us as a perfect, beautiful boy. It was difficult for us to choose a name for him. We were at a complete loss. Our good friends who are not believers were visiting us one day and asked us if we had a name for our upcoming baby. Our dear friend Stacie who is like an aunt to our children, suggested the name Joshua because she thought it sounded cute with the name Jacob. Since we couldn't come up with anything better, my husband and I agreed. This time, we didn't spend much time looking up religious names or themes. All we knew was that Joshua meant "He saves." What he saved from, we had no idea.

God is sovereign and amazing in the way He works within our lives. We have hints of His divine presence, but we somehow fail to notice them in our everyday rush. When God chose the name Joshua for our son, he was pointing the way to His Son. We were so caught up in our lives that we completely missed it. We did not have the eyes to see.

Years later, when we were all preparing to be baptized, our associate pastor asked me about the children's names again. So I told him: Jacob, Joshua and Sarah (yes, we got our Sarah finally after years of waiting). He chuckled as if he was privy to an inside joke and then asked me "who picked the name for Joshua?" I told him that it was our close family friend. He asked if they were a Christian believer and I said didn't think she was. He then told me something so very profound. He said that "Joshua" is the Greek version of "Yeshua." Yeshua was Jesus' original name in Hebrew. Both mean "He Saves."

Putting these names together allows me to see God's presence in our family's life and how He has guided my spiritual transformation. In the beginning of my search, I struggled with Islam and with God (Jacob). He allowed me to wrestle with these notions and touched my life in a significant way that I could not deny His providence for me. This led to my acceptance that Christ Jesus was my Lord and I was saved by Him (Joshua). Now, I am adopted into His family of believers and am considered to be a part of the royal priesthood of believers (1 Peter 2:9). This makes me his princess (Sarah).

It is awe-inspiring to see God at work. He took a sideline Christian and a Muslim woman and gave their children powerful names from His book. He had pointed us to Christ even back before we had any idea we were seekers. God's hand was evident in choosing names for our babies. Our own names and the names of our children are written on the palms of His hands (Isaiah 49:16).

Chapter 4

Faced With 9/11

L iving in California was like being on a treadmill. You were constantly running and didn't know when you were going to get off because the days melted into one another without much to show for them. We had been married for seven years now and Stephen's parents had moved to Oklahoma for his father's work. Our vacation trips to Oklahoma to visit his family brought us unexpected peace. The pace of life was slower, people were nicer and no one seemed to be in a hurry for anything.

I was not excited about the prospect of having two children in daycare and was tired of working. We decided that the cost of living in Oklahoma would be better for us and that maybe there we could survive on one income. We moved to Oklahoma in November of 2000. We were able to buy a very nice home that was almost double the space of our home in California. Of course, my father and mother were very sad and upset that a part of their family had now moved away.

Ten months after our move, the events of September 11 took place. There was so much confusion for the entire country as the media showed repeated clips of airplanes crashing into the Twin Towers in New York City. Everyone was questioning what happened. Why would people do something like this? Would this be a one-time event or were more attacks planned for the United States?

I was working as a Human Resources consultant and did training for companies. Several started to call me due to my unique background and experience living in the Middle East. Also, I was a Muslim woman who was outspoken and I really didn't mind working with companies to help them understand religious views and diversity. Many people ask me if I was targeted after 9/11 or profiled unfairly. They are surprised when I tell them that 9/11 was actually fairly profitable for me, as I gained popularity as a paid professional speaker who was candid about her cultural Muslim beliefs.

There was one event in particular when I was hired by a group of non-profit lawyers to come and speak to them about my past, heritage, culture and religion. After I spoke to them, they started to hammer me with questions about the Quran. They said that I had presented Islam in glowing terms to them. Then one asked whether the Quran specifically stated that the actions of the 9/11 terrorists were not just sanctioned, but encouraged? Another asked: Didn't the Quran state that women's role was to behave in a certain way?

Another fired off a stronger question: Didn't the Quran have some harsh teachings about dealing with Infidels or those who held beliefs in opposition to Islam? I was floored. I did not have the answers for a very simple reason. I had never read the Quran. I told the group the truth that I had never read the Quran, but promised them that I would research and get back to them with the answers.

I was not alone in my lack of knowledge of the Quran. Many in the Islamic world are ignorant of what is in their book. The main reason for this ignorance is not time or money. It is language. In order to read the Quran, you must read it in Arabic. According to the Quran, Arabic is the language of Heaven. God will only speak to you in that language and when you pray, you must speak to Him in that tongue. There are Muslims from many countries who do not read or write in Arabic. In fact, the number of Muslim countries that speak Arabic is limited to the Middle East and Egypt.

I remember being a little girl around eight or nine years old and my grandmother was trying to teach me how to pray. All prayers are also recited in Arabic and out of the several languages I spoke already, Arabic was not one of them. I vividly recall my father reading his Engineering magazine one evening. I walked in and sat by his feet. I looked at him and asked "Daddy, how many languages do you speak?" This is something my father has always prided himself upon. He has told us many times that his love for languages has served him well over the years. He stopped reading and answered "Well, I speak over six languages: I speak English, Urdu,

Punjabi, Arabic, German and Farsi." I looked at him again and asked him "Daddy, if you speak over six languages, then why does God only speak **one**?"

Even as a little girl, I knew that it made no sense that God would demand that we speak to him in a language we did not understand. Why was the unlimited God of the Universe limited in this one thing that even humans had the capacity to overcome? It made absolutely no sense to me. As a Christian, I smiled when I found out that when the Holy Spirit came to the believers at Pentecost in Acts 2, they started to speak in different tongues. The very last language group listed is Arabs (Acts 2:11). This proved to me that God spoke and understood all languages - not just one!

Nevertheless, I opted to make good on my promise to the questioning lawyers and delve into a deep study of the Quran. It also made good business sense that if I was going to go be paid to speak about Islam, I should know what I was talking about. Since I was not about to take a Rosetta Stone crash course in the Arabic language, I decided that the Quran my father gave me on my wedding day with the English translation by Yusaf Ali would be a good place to start.

I started at the beginning. The Quran is not organized according to revelation to Prophet Mohammad (his name is also written as Muhammad), but is arranged from the longest Surah (chapter) to the shortest. This makes for such confusing reading! It's not like picking up the Bible and flipping to a story like Daniel in the lion's den. You can read the Bible to a three year old child and they would understand the storyline. Instead, the Quran is a series of revelations. According to tradition, when the Prophet Mohammad would have a revelation, he would start to shake, sometimes foam at the mouth and he would say "cover me." The revelations he had were even scary to him, as he shared with his first wife, Khadija. The Quran even mentions "Yet they turn away from him and say: "Tutored (by others), a man possessed!" - Surah 44:14 (Yusuf Ali) and also here "And say: "What! shall we give up our gods for the sake of a Poet possessed (or in another translation "a mad Poet")?" Surah 37:36 (Yusuf Ali).

The uttering when Mohammad was covered are what were then written down as revelation from God to the angel Gabriel who told him to read and then to Mohammad[2]. According to the dictionary, the word "Quran" (sometimes written as "Koran" - both proper forms and spelling) means "recited word or recitation" in Arabic. It is believed that Mohammad and his followers both wrote down the messages from God.

Even the Quran mentions this in Surah Al Isra 17:106 "And [it is] a Quran which we have separated [by intervals] that you might recite it to the people over a prolonged period. And we have sent it down progressively" The Quran was written on branches of trees, on leaves, on conserved bits of paper, animal skins and bones. It was written down but not organized at all. It was later collected after

---

[2] http://www.al-islam.org/restatement-history-islam-and-muslims-sayyid-ali-ashgar-razwy/birth-islam-and-proclamation-muhammad

many years and was finally organized into a book of recitations.

The names of the chapters within the Quran are also striking. Some of the titles of Surahs are "The Cow, The Ants, The Moon, The Iron, The Pen, The Clot, The Women, and The Jinn." Jinn are interesting spiritual beings that are believed to be half man, half fire and are usually mischievous by nature. They are believed to have supernatural powers and some may even consider them to be impish, evil spirits or little devils. The book's organization makes things very hard to follow. For example, you could be reading about a great conquest made by the Prophet Mohammad and guidelines to divide up the spoils, and then the next chapter tells you about how Solomon had command over the winds, traveled for one day and covered distance that would take over a month, he had a spring of liquid copper and finally that the Jinn were ordered by God to work for him. (Surah Saba 34:12). The part about Solomon was contained all in one verse.

In addition, some of the Surahs start with Arabic Letters like "Alif, Laam, Meem" (equivalent of the English letters A, L, M) but no one in the Islamic world knows what they mean or why they are there. Before I get too deeply into the confusion, I also want to point out that there is also an equally as confusing term in the Bible that many have not figured out. It's the term "Selah" that shows up mainly in the Psalms and also in Habakkuk. No one really knows why that's there either - as there are mysteries in each book.

There were two chapters that stood out to me in the Quran. The first one was called Surah 4 "Al Nisa'" or The Women. This chapter is written mainly for men and contains instructions on how to marry, rules on inheritance for men and women (they can only get half portion after the men in the family get their full portions), divorce, children and also female slaves. The disturbing part of reading this chapter was that my older sister was in the process of getting a divorce from her husband - which is forbidden in Islam. He did not treat her with respect or kindness and she was truly an American, who was used to having certain freedoms that even our own parents allowed. As I mentioned before, my parents are highly educated, progressive and with three daughters, they have always held a higher view of women's rights than that found many in Islamic nations.

According to the Surah Al Nisa, the way he was treating her was sanctioned. The Quran allows for beating a wife. It also allows for multiple marriages. There is apparently nothing wrong with a man exchanging wives or having a slave as a wife even if she is already married to another. (Surah Al Nisa 4:20 and 4:24). Since this was the first time I had ever read anything like this, I couldn't believe it was true. This is a horrible thing for a Muslim to do! The tough part to understand here is that a Muslim person has to believe one hundred percent of what the Quran states. Even if you question something little or say maybe you are not sure you believe it, you are no longer a Muslim at that point. Unless you believe that every word of the

Quran is divine revelation from God, you cannot be a Muslim.

The freedom that Christians have to openly debate, question, and disagree about things in the Bible are taken for granted by many. An average Muslim person is absolutely terrified of entering into a questioning phase when it comes to the Quran. Many elders (Imams, scholars and parents) consider it to be rude at the least and some say it is ultimate blasphemy if you question them or the Quran. The culture also dictates a certain respect and submission to authority, so not only is it a religious issue, but also a cultural faux pas to question.

Given all this, I called the only person who I thought would entertain my questions about this chapter. I called my mother and told her that I had just started reading the Quran to become a better Muslim and that I needed her help. She sounded genuinely interested and asked how she could help me in this endeavor. When I started asking her questions about my brother-in-law's treatment of my sister, she became quiet and I could hear anger in her voice as it shook. She asked me why I was questioning the Quran and if I thought it would be okay for him to treat her that way. Of course, I did not agree with his treatment. I thought he was pompous and self-centered from the beginning. I was only questioning why God would allow half of his creation to be treated in this manner. Were women really worth half of a man (Surah Al Nisa 4:11)?

Chapter 5

Isa in the Quran

I continued to make my way through the odd chapters, trying to piece together what God had intended to be my purpose as a Muslim woman. Since the Quran is written mainly with men in mind as the audience, it has little to say about any role a woman may have in furthering God's agenda. That role seems to be reserved for men only, with women's role revolving around pleasing their husband and dealing with childbirth.

It should be noted that the Quran gives full chapters to a few of the Biblical prophets: Jonah, Joseph, and Abraham. Moses is mentioned mainly in the Surah called "The Cow." Other figures from the Bible also mentioned in the Quran: Adam, Moses, Aaron, Lot, Solomon, David, Jacob, Isaac, Noah, Job, Ishmael, Elisha, and amazingly enough, Zacharias and his son, John the Baptist (Yahya in Arabic).

There is only ONE woman named in the entire Quran. Not even the prophet Mohammad's favored wife is named. It is Maryam, or Mary - Jesus Christ's mother. There is an entire chapter devoted to Jesus (named Isa [pronounced "ee-saw"] in Arabic- taken presumably from the Greek "Iesous") titled Maryam and is found in Surah 19. This is the first time I had ever read anything about the life of Jesus. Muslims know generalities about Isa but are not encouraged to learn about Him, while Abraham and other prophets are a part of normal conversation and even daily prayer recitations for Muslims.

As a child, I grew up knowing that Muslims revere Prophet Isa. In fact, upon moving to the United States, I often heard my parents in conversations with Westerners who might bring up religion. Some say that they respect Isa and are taught to revere him as one of the more important prophets of God. In fact, my family is one of many Muslim families who believe that "one who sits on the right hand of God will come to judge" on judgment day as Jesus!

(And he shall be a sign for (the coming of) the Hour.) means, sign and "One of the signs of the Hour will be the appearance of `Isa son of Maryam before the Day of Resurrection." Something similar was also narrated from Abu Hurayrah, Ibn `Abbas, `Abu Al-`Aliyah, Abu Malik, `Ikrimah, Al-Hasan, Qatadah, Ad-Dahhak and others. Many Mutawatir Hadiths report that the Messenger of Allah said that `**Isa will descend before the Day of Resurrection as a just ruler and fair judge.** *(Tafsir Ibn Kathir[3]).*

---

[3]http://www.qtafsir.com/index.php?option=com_content&task=view&id=2076&Itemid=99

The chapter on Jesus really threw my Muslim mind into a loop. The Quran itself attests to the divine nature of Jesus Christ's birth. ALL Muslims believe that he was born of the Virgin Mary and that God willed it to be so. I have actually met several Christians who have doubts or flatly reject the virgin birth, while no Muslim would ever doubt this to not be the truth. The next thing the Quran states may be apocryphal, where Jesus as a young boy makes clay figures of birds, blows his breath into them and the birds miraculously fly away. There is not an exhaustive list of Jesus's miracles, but several miracles are recognized such as curing blindness, leprosy and raising people from the dead (Quran Surah 3:49).

Jesus also died with miraculous occurrences in the Quran. The Quran specifically states that the people did not kill him nor was he crucified.

> And [We cursed them] for their disbelief and their saying against Mary a great slander, and [for] their saying, "Indeed, we have killed the Messiah, Jesus, the son of Mary, the messenger of Allah." And they did not kill him nor did they crucify him; but [another] was made to resemble him to them. And indeed, those who differ over it are in doubt about it. They have no knowledge of it except the following of assumption. And they did not kill him, for certain. Rather, Allah raised him to Himself. And ever is Allah Exalted in Might and Wise. (Quran Surah 4:156-158).

So, reading this text as a Muslim, I became very intrigued. If the life of Jesus was covered in such detail, wouldn't the life of God's favored prophet be even more spectacular? I only knew bits and pieces of Mohammad's life, but never really looked further than what I was told by my parents or what I had learned at the Mosque during our infrequent visits.

I picked up the phone again and called my mother. I told her that I had gotten further in my study of the Quran and was excited to talk to her about prophet Mohammad. So I launched into my questions: Isa was born of a divine miracle, so how was prophet Mohammad born? My mom told me that he was an orphan, as his parents died when he was young and that he was raised by his uncle Abu Talib. All of this I had already known, so I pressed my mom for more details. She really didn't have much more information to give me than that.

I went on to my next question: Isa performed so many miracles - giver of life, healed the blind, and other diseases, had power over demons, had power over death. So, where are the miracles of Mohammad's life recorded in the Quran. My mother got very excited over this one and she said "Well, he did the biggest miracle of all! He wrote the Quran." Knowing that all Muslims believe in God's four books: the Torah given to Moses, the Psalms given to David, the Injeel or Gospels given to Jesus and the Quran given to Mohammad, I found that response to be slightly lacking. I asked my mom that the other three prophets also had books credited to their names, so why was this so special? My mom told me that the reason that was the greatest miracle achieved by a prophet is because the Quran was given to Mohammad in its entirety and it is God's final word on earth. He will no longer speak to any other human.

Undeterred by this, I went on to my final questioning. Why did Allah raise Isa off the cross and take him straight to heaven? That was pretty amazing that Muslims believe that Jesus didn't even die. So, did Mohammad have an equally amazing ending to his life on earth? There was a long silence on the other end of the line as I waited for my mom to process what I was asking. She said one word, "Pneumonia." I repeated "Pneumonia?" What do you mean? She said "He died of Pneumonia." I was horrified! How could God allow the seal of prophets, his most favored to die from a common disease? How embarrassing! My mom said "Wait, wait! There's another line of thought for this. Some Muslims believe that he was poisoned!" "Poisoned?" I repeated incredulously. "That's even worse! That means others had power over him and killed him!" I just sat there in disbelief and another thought popped into my head. "Mom, Isn't Isa the one who comes back to judge on judgment day?" I know that she was panicking at that point. But to her credit, she said "Yes. We believe that." I then asked "So where is Prophet Mohammad in all this? Why is Jesus so special? If he is to judge me, shouldn't I be on his team? Wouldn't he give me some sort of extra credit for that?"

My parents are not the only Muslims who believe that Jesus

Christ will return to earth on judgment day. There are several hadiths that are available to read that attest to the fact that Christ will descend as a just judge (Sahih Muslim, Book 001, Number 0289[4] and Sahih al-Bukhari, Volume 3, Book 43, Number 656[5]).

Since everything a Muslim believes is based on works, it's not out of line to think of performing religious duties as transactions or extra credit. When talking to my mother, I actually meant that God would look upon me favorably if I somehow associated myself more with Jesus, but as I gave that notion further thought, I resolved that the notion was just plain silly - Muslims could not be associated with Jesus. That was reserved for Christians.

At the end of the phone call, my mom then gave me the best advice I have had in my life. She told me that she was truly frightened that I was possessed by the devil and his evil spirits were confusing me when I was reading the Quran. She told me to set the Quran aside and ask God. He was the author of all His books and so He would be the best one to answer all my questions. She told me also that "Seek the truth from God and He will show you the way." I realized much later that she almost quoted John 14:6 without knowing "I am the way, the truth, and the life. No one comes to the Father except through Me."

---

[4] http://hadithcollection.com/sahihbukhari/129-sahih-muslim/Sahih%20Muslim%20Book%2001.%20Faith/8495-sahih-muslim-book-001-hadith-number-0289.html
[5] https://muflihun.com/bukhari/43/656

Chapter 6

Go to Church!

Around the same time as I was studying the Quran, I knew we should have another child. It was so hard to explain the feeling I had - it was as if our family was incomplete. In fact, I told my husband very tearfully that I felt a baby was waiting for us in heaven - just waiting to be born. Our feelings on this were most definitely not aligned. In fact, he was quite certain that God did not want us to have another child and that he was content with two beautiful boys that he had blessed us with already.

So, I did as any good Muslim wife would... I prayed. I prayed fervently to God for five years. Now mind you, this might be a bit longer than the average wait time for a child, but I had a long fuse - or so I thought. After asking my husband once a year whether or not he had changed his mind about having a third child, he told me "no" year after year. When it was the fifth year, I asked my husband if he had reconsidered. He looked at me seriously and said that he was truly sorry. He had not and would not change his mind. He was perfectly happy with his two boys.

That night, I prayed the absolute worst prayer of my life. In the Muslim world, all prayers have to meet a set standard of rakats in each prayer. A rakat is a set standard of verses and movements that go with each of the five prayers per day. After you meet these required rakats, tradition is that you can then sit and ask God for what you want or you can say some extra credit prayers (according to rakat requirements) in case you messed up something during prayer or needed something extra from God.

The prayer I prayed would have been absolutely rejected by any Muslim Imam. In fact, I would have been chastised for praying it! I simply sat down by my bed, on my feet and told God what I thought of praying to Him for the last five years. I was so incredibly furious! I had been praying for five years and I had nothing to show from it. He did not give me what I had wanted, so basically I told God that I quit. I would not pray to Him about this matter anymore and through my angry tears, I told Him that I guess it was His will that we would only have two children. At least I got that part right - as a Muslim, you have to submit to Allah's will because He is the one who decides what He will bless you with and what He will not give to you. I felt very cheated by God because when you pray, you are doing it to gain credit with God. If you do X, you should get Y. Treating God as a vending machine was not a good idea and it bordered on being blasphemous. When I put my religious coins in and did not receive anything in return, I started to kick and scream like a child at not getting things my way. The ironic part is that Muslims are taught to believe in destiny set by Allah, so after I got over my anger, I realized that maybe I should just accept and walk away.

Two weeks later, my husband came home exhausted from work. On this night, he looked incredibly thoughtful and quiet. After dinner, he asked me "do you still want another child?" I stared at him in disbelief. Not happiness, but real indignation. How dare he mock me in this manner, when I had been asking him for the last five stinking years? I thought he was joking with me and I did not find it funny in the least. When I stopped and looked at him, he didn't look like he was teasing me at all. In fact, he stayed calm as I railed at him in exasperation. Of course I still wanted a child but had resolved myself to the fact that it was not in Allah's will that we had another one.

He then told me about something that happened to him that day. He said that he went to set up medical equipment for an elderly lady at her home. She had pictures of her children in the hallway and there was a portrait of a lovely young girl and a handsome boy. When he asked about her children, she got visibly upset and through her tears, she told him that one of her children had died in a car accident. She said that now, she only has one child and oh, how she had begged her husband to have three children! My husband said that he couldn't bear it! At once, he thought of how I had asked him over and over again for another child and he could not bear to be the one to not give me what I had wanted for so long. He said that he could see how the woman had not forgiven her husband for this one failing.

Instantly, I was overjoyed! I knew without a shadow of doubt that this was God's doing. I knew that somehow, He had heard my prayers. I still thought there might be more to this, so I told him that we could wait a month so that he could be sure about this decision (I had waited this long, might as well wait another thirty days). He told me that he was sure. We didn't have to wait.

It had been six years since we had Joshua. It took us some time to have a baby with each one, so of course I could not expect to be pregnant straightaway. I quickly found out that I was pregnant right away! Immediately, I gave that praise to God. Within months, we found out that we were having a girl. Again, I gave that praise to God. Not only did He give me the desire of my heart, but He wrapped her up in a big pink bow! I was overwhelmed.

I started praying fervently for God to show me how I could re-pay Him. In Islam, nothing happens without a string attached. God demands for you to do something in return because there is no grace. My parents also encouraged me to give to charity (zakat or giving of alms) so that I would not bring about an evil eye or omen on this pregnancy. If you don't thank God properly, the Muslim superstition is that an evil eye could be upon you. So with this thought in mind, I asked God to tell how I could pay off this precious debt to Him.

Just a few months prior to this, my mother had told me to set the Quran down and pray for God to show me His truth. So I thought that yes, this would be a good time to ask him again to show me the way I could do something for Him. In just a few days, I had my answer.

"GO TO CHURCH."

I woke up one morning with this strange thought rattling around my mind. I knew that I was still in the sleep/awake haze of the morning, but as I tried to clear my head I could still envision the words "GO TO CHURCH." My only thought in response was "Hmmm... that's weird." I completely forgot about it and went on with my business. That night, after I prayed for God to show me how I could thank Him and I was falling asleep, I suddenly came upon the thought "GO TO CHURCH" again in my head. I actually shook my head to dispel it and eventually, I drifted off to sleep. In the morning, it was "GO TO CHURCH" again. How very annoying! What on earth could that mean?

Of course, I rationalized, that it couldn't possibly be a message for me from God. He would NEVER tell a Muslim person to go to church. That would simply be ridiculous. I actually chuckled at the absurdity of it as I was preparing dinner for my family that evening. Nevertheless, that night, it was "GO TO CHURCH" again.

Morning, night, morning, night, it was "GO TO CHURCH," "GO TO CHURCH," "GO TO CHURCH." I found that the more I tried to dismiss or rationalize the message, the more intense it got. At one point, I found that it was an actual voice, echoing in my head. I had to make this stop or I felt like I would truly go insane. Once more, I rationalized that "maybe it's pregnancy hormones? I think I read somewhere that they make some women nutty."

Obsessed with this thought, one evening, I suddenly came to a solution! The message MUST be for my husband who was a Christian! Surely God wanted him to go to church! I was sure that was the case. So as he was drifting off to sleep, I told him that I thought God had given me a message for him. I told him that God wanted him to go to church. He crinkled up his eyes in confusion and said "If God has a message for me, why doesn't he ask me Himself?" I thought that was an entirely rude way to answer someone who has a message from heaven. I told him that I believed God wanted him to go to church for quite a long time. Besides, we had agreed before we were even married that we would raise our children as Christians in the Church. Again, he politely informed me that God had said no such message for him and that maybe, it was meant for me. Well, that was absolutely ridiculous! God would not ask such a thing of a Muslim woman and with that final comment, I turned off the bedside light.

Again, it was "GO TO CHURCH" rattling around in my head. Only now, the message was emblazoned on a huge marquee with lights blinking on and off (or so it seemed). The message was not going away. So, I thought with some desperation that if it wasn't for my husband, maybe it's for the kids! YES! That must be the case. But how do I get them to church?

The answer came in just a few days. I was sitting on a bench for the boys' summer baseball practice when a woman asked me if the boys were enrolled in any VBS programs that summer. I had no clue what she was talking about. She said "You know, VBS?" I told her I had not the faintest idea of what that was. She asked "Do you live in Oklahoma? How do you not know what that is - the signs are posted all around town at every church! It's Vacation Bible School." Again... no clue what that was. She pushed out an exasperated breath and said "It's basically where you take your kids for a week, they learn about God, they play, they get a free T-shirt and they even get a free meal. You can just drop them off and go shopping!" It sounded too good to be true to me, so I asked where I could sign up. I went home immediately and jumped on the computer. It turned out that this was the first (and only) year the church had tried online sign-ups for VBS and so I was able to print out a confirmation for enrollment at the First Presbyterian Church of Edmond Summer VBS.

At the Saturday game, I thanked the woman for telling me about VBS and that I had my confirmation already to go. She looked surprised as she told me that she was not able to enroll her children as of that Friday and they were on a waiting list (turns out that the church had over 300 kids signed up that year!). Thinking "too bad for you," I was pretty happy that my children got in so I could have that annoying message go away because now I would be taking my boys to church. It made perfect sense that would be God's will.

VBS was fine, since I drove my children there, jumped out and jumped back into the car as quickly as I could without talking to anyone. However, the final day was on Friday. Jacob's teacher stopped me at the classroom door and began to talk to me. She asked some very pleasant, general questions and then she asked me if I had a church family. I courteously told her I did not. She told me briefly about this church and mistaking my silence for interest, she asked me if I would like to meet the pastor. Without even waiting for my answer, she grabbed my hand and marched me through a maze of hallways and stairs into a large, wood-paneled office. Along the way, as I protested and tried to take my hand back, she told me that he wouldn't be there anyway, since the pastors were off on Fridays. Of course, he was there. He was reclining in his chair with a book, wearing a T-shirt and casual pants. Until now, I had only seen a Catholic priest at a very formal Hispanic wedding and this man was absolutely not dressed like the priest had been.

He looked up with interest, motioned me to his table and asked me to sit down. I remained standing. the VBS teacher made hasty introductions and told the pastor that I may have been considering a church. I immediately told him that I was not. He seemed confused by this, so he asked "well, then do you know of anyone who might be considering a church?" The only thing that came to my tongue was a lie. I told him that "yes, my husband is." I am sure he was even more confused by that comment. He then smiled gently and asked me what type of a church my husband looking for? Since I had lied and had never had this conversation with my spouse, I had to think quickly. The first thing that popped into my head was that his family was fairly conservative. I didn't even know if churches were conservative or liberal or whatever. He seemed to be okay with that answer and told me that this church was as conservative as Presbyterian churches could be. "What else is he looking for?" I was proud of having a decent answer for the first time and he looked so intent on another answer that I blurted out "He doesn't like hugs."

A legend in my husband's side of the family goes something like this: His parents decided to check out some churches in Oklahoma. They went to several that were either too big or too small or too weird. They went to a smallish Presbyterian church and everyone hugged them as soon as they walked in the doors. The horror in my father-in-law's eyes when he described people descending on them sent shivers down my husband's spine. "I hope I never have something like that happen to me," he told me afterwards. So, that's the only file my mind pulled as an adequate answer to that question. I saw a faint smile come across the pastor's kind face. He stood up and told me "Tell your husband that we are a conservative, non-hugging church and that I personally invite him to attend this Sunday. Besides, the kids will have a VBS program, so it would be a good time to visit."

At the dinner table that night, I waited until dessert to bring up the day's events. I told my husband "Hey! The pastor at the First Presbyterian Church personally invited you to attend this Sunday!" I was met with nothing but silence. "Do you think you want to go?" He looked up from his plate and said "What are you talking about? Why were you talking to a pastor? Where is this church?" I told him very casually that the kids had been going that week to VBS (he didn't know what that meant either) and that they would have a small program for the children, but that the pastor wanted to meet him and he had a personal invitation.

In the eastern culture, when someone issues a personal invitation, it is to be taken very seriously. The gravity of the situation is emphasized when a man of God invites you personally. I told him that he had to go - no choice in the matter. He shook his head and said "He's a pastor. It's his JOB to invite people to come to his church - it's what they do. They don't really mean it." I could tell I was losing this argument. So I had to play the crying wife card. I broke down in tears and told him that someone from this family is supposed to GO TO CHURCH and since my Christian husband wasn't doing it, that I took the kids and now the pastor wanted to meet him and that would be very sinful if he turned down a man of God. Even if the pastor didn't notice that he declined his invitation, God would count it against us as a sin. Knowing that this was a losing battle, he folded his arms and said "Okay, I'll go if you go."

Go to Church!

For the first time in my life, I stepped into church for a Sunday service. I had no idea what to expect. It was very scary to me. Everyone looked different, knew each other, knew when to respond to the person talking, knew when to sing and stand up. This was completely different than anything in the mosque. Since I was wallowing in my own pity of a Muslim having to come to church, I didn't notice my poor husband crowding around me, and wanting to sit in the furthest, darkest corner we could find. Of course, he did emphasize to me on the way to church "No one better hug me. One touch and I'm out the door!"

We made it through the service without being touched. He was quickly headed out the door when I said "You haven't met the pastor yet!" So we made it all the way down to the front (it was a big church with many pews) and I introduced the pastor to my husband. In the car on the way back home, he said "well, that wasn't too bad."

While we were waiting for the service to begin, I had noticed announcements on the overhead screen. One of the announcements was for a New Member's class. Since he didn't think church was too bad, I thought I would tell him that they were accepting new members. "Churches are ALWAYS accepting new members, Mona! This is the first time I have stepped inside a church since we've been married. I am not ready for this and I am definitely not about to become a new member!" I look back at this exchange and think about how scared he must have been about not just attending a new church but now being pressured into membership. I didn't realize this can be a long process for some people as they take years to commit to a church. Yet here we were signing up within days.

As I thought about it more over the week, I reasoned that he might want to know more about being a new member so I called the church. They told me that the new member class had already started, but only one week had gone by. They were sure that we could join in. So I gave them his contact information and apparently they contacted him because he told me "What have you done? They know my name and have my information now." Since the husband always takes the religious lead in a Muslim family, I told him that if the message was for the kids to GO TO CHURCH, that he needed to be the one to take them. If he was going to go to church, he should probably become a new member. As he listened to my line of logic, he folded his arms and said "Okay, I'll go if you go."

Well, that was just funny and so ridiculous. I knew that my attending service and praying my own Muslim prayers at church was vastly different than becoming a member. I knew enough to know that no church would ever allow a Muslim to be a member. I told him that the church would never accept me and said I would go only to support him. I would be quiet and just sit to listen.

We showed up to the new members class and I was handed a notebook along with a book called "How to Spell Presbyterian" by James Angell. I knew I didn't need either one of those things. They also gave a set to my husband and he actually seemed interested in what they were saying. Another pastor came in to speak about the Bible. He started off with the Trinity. This is something I had never heard or thought about. He held up a glass and said "The Trinity is like a glass of ice water. All three phases are there at the same time. You cannot tell when solid ice becomes liquid or vaporizes into the air. Jesus is like the ice you can see. God is like the water, immersing everything and the Holy Spirit is like the vapor coming off the ice. All three are distinct, yet one."

I was so confused. I raised my hand and said "So according to what you're saying, Jesus is God?" He said yes, thanked me for making his point and went on lecturing. For me, so great was this blasphemy that I wanted to take both of my hands and cover my ears! I could not be a witness to this nor could I sit there in class, pretending like he didn't just violate everything I had been reading in the Quran about God being only one. But God being three? Never. God being Jesus? I couldn't even process that thought. It was inconceivable.

I told my husband that I could not be a part of the class anymore because of what the pastor said. He was so unschooled in Christian beliefs that he told me "That's not what he said." I told him that was indeed what he said and I took down notes to prove it. "That's not what he meant, then" was his response. With my arms crossed and my cheeks red from displeasure, I didn't have to say anything in reply. "Let's go again and ask him. If he says that's true then we won't go there again." This was from my husband who didn't want to go to church in the first place. Now he was trying to convince me to go to class again.

The next Sunday morning was bleak. There was heavy thunder as the Oklahoma sky had opened up to pour down rain. There were threatening black clouds, as dark as my mood at being made to go and hear blasphemy against my God again. I was not happy. We showed up to our small group of eight people and looked around at the empty room. How many showed that morning? You guessed it!

TWO.

Chapter 7

Jesus Christ Makes Sense

Oh, I was fuming mad! Not only was I not interested in coming to church but on this bleak day with no one there from the group. Where were all the Christians? It was rotten luck and my gut reaction was to just leave. No one would know, notice or care and if they did... so what? Alone I stood in the empty small group room, since my husband stopped to get a drink of water or use the restroom. Our group leader, sauntered in with a sunny smile. I looked at him and spilled out a hateful confession. I told him "I need you to know a few things." All of a sudden, his smile disappeared. "I'm a fraud. I am not a Christian, nor do I ever plan to be. I am a Muslim and in fact, have been trying to be a better Muslim for the last few years. I don't belong here. When the pastor mentioned that we would write a paper on our Christian life, I planned to turn in a blank paper. I don't have a Christian life and don't want one. I don't want to be here and I think you need to know this." With an exhale, I felt much better all of a sudden. It was a great relief to get that burden off my chest. The group leader, on the other hand, didn't look so good. He did not say a word to me. Instead, he began to say something, hesitated, turned on his heel and walked out of the room.

Stephen came back and looked around as if to ask if we were still meeting since the room remained empty. I told him that our leader had just stopped by but I did not know what he was doing. As we sat down in the empty circle of chairs, the teaching pastor walked in (you know, the ice water one). He sat down with the group leader and looked at us. With a deep breath and a concerned expression, he began by saying "Well, sometimes our spouses make us do things we don't want to do, like come to church." My husband replied back quickly "I know."

The pastor's forehead furrowed in confusion. "I said, that sometimes our spouses force us into something we don't want to do." Again, Stephen replied "Yes, I know. You're right." The pastor again looked confused and asked Stephen "Are you Muslim?" He looked a little affronted by the question and said "No, I'm Christian."

"Okay, so when I said that our spouses make us come to church, who forced whom?"

"Oh, my wife made me come."

Looking at me, he asked "You are a Christian?"

"No, I'm Muslim."

He shook his head at this point and then asked "You made your Christian husband come to church?

"Yes, because he wouldn't go and I know God wants him to!"

"Do you want to be here?"

"NO!"

Stephen interrupted by saying "Well, I don't want to be here either!"

The pastor sat back in his chair and asked me "why are you here?"

To which my reply was to burst into tears.

He then said "This is too much for today. Would both of you be willing to take out a little time during this week to meet with me in my office? I just want to talk to you about what is going on." Miraculously, we agreed to meet with him that Wednesday evening.

When Wednesday came, the pastor was ready for us. He used to be a Petroleum Engineer and that training stayed with him, since he had a T-chart on his dry erase board with "Islam" on one side and a "Cross" on the other side. Eagerly, he ushered us into his office and asked us to sit down on the couch. He didn't waste any time at all by saying "tell me what are the five pillars of faith for Islam."

I was surprised that I was being given a test. Nevertheless, I answered with the first and most important - Belief in ONE God (Shahada). He wrote it down and then asked "Do you believe in One God?" I remember thinking, what a silly question to ask a Muslim. That's by definition - you have to believe that "*There is no god but Allah. Muhammad is the messenger of God (la ilaha illa'llah. Muhammadun rasul Allah).*" This is the Islamic creed or testimony. You have to say this in front of another Muslim (or multiple Muslims) and immediately, you become a Muslim. There is nothing else you have to do. When babies are born, the Shahada is recited into their ear so that they are claimed for Islam. My dad recited the Shahada in our ears when we were born and also in both of our sons' ears in the hospital. It is one of the things that is included in the call to prayer in Muslim countries. This is a statement of faith and is the only requirement to belong to the Muslim community of faith. "Of course I do" was my answer. He placed a checkmark by the first pillar or faith and then said "Next?"

I replied with - Prayers five times a day (Salat or Salah). He asked "Do you pray five times a day?" This one was more difficult to answer. I had been on this journey to become a better Muslim and praying five times a day was a detriment to me. I had always been taught that there was no intermediary between God and a Muslim, so this was the way you could get closer to God. As I mentioned earlier in the book, there are assigned times for prayer and a format that needs to fit each time you pray. The prayers are to be said at certain times of the day, with Arabic verses that go with each prayer (rakat) and need to be completed with ablutions (washing to purify) to even be able to pray. Given that I couldn't get up before dawn, complete the requisite washings, say my prayers in Arabic, get ready for work, make breakfast and get children ready for school -- all this for just the early morning prayer... I was not doing too well. During the day, when you have to work and teach, you can't just leave what you are doing in order to throw down a prayer mat and start praying. It was very limiting. There is a simple reference chart made for children on how to do all this at Islamweb's Kids Corner[6].

So, my answer was "I try to pray five times a day, but sometimes it doesn't work out for me." He replied "Oh, that's too bad" and crossed off the second requirement. "Next?" Well, next comes the giving of alms or charity (Zaka). Zakat[7] in Arabic means purification and also growth for a Muslim. In the Quran, Zakat is called "Sadaqatt." The Surah Tauba 9:103 states "(O Mohammed) take out of their possessions Sadaqat so that you may cleanse and purify them thereby, and pray for them..." Many Muslims (including my parents and their Sunni tradition) choose to give 2.5% of their income for Zakat, but this is not stated very clearly (some say it is not stated at all) in the Quran[8]. A rule of thumb is that a person should give whatever they feel like giving. If an occasion called for a large gift of charity, you could do that or a small one for a friend. It is up to you on what you wish to give. According to the National Foundation[9] for Zakat, Zakat is sometimes (not always) given out of guilt as an offering to make up for lack of fasting, lying or cheating. So, it's not always clear why charity is being given - other than as a requirement. In the past, I had given charity both for guilt as well as thanksgiving. I was confident in this pillar of faith, as my husband and I had given charity to the mosque my family was

---

6 http://www.islamweb.net/kidsen/Kids%20Corner%201,2/subjects/salah2.html
7 http://www.islam-guide.com/ch3-16.htm#footnote1
8 see http://islamqa.info/en/145600
9 http://www.nzf.org.uk/Knowledge/ObjectiveOfZakat

associated with in Lodi, California. We also donated money to other things such as fundraisers and non-religious charities. This was a good one, so I said yes confidently. "Next?" he asked after putting another checkmark on the board.

Fasting (Sawm) is the fourth pillar of Islam. Sawm doesn't have to be done at Ramadan and a Muslim can fast at any time. Fasting during Ramadan, however, is mandatory and expected according to Islamic law. Surah Al Baqara 2:183 says "Believers! Fasting is enjoined upon you, as it was enjoined upon those before you, that you become God-fearing." At first, Muhammad called all Muslims to fast at least three days a month outside of Ramadan. That rule was later relaxed and allowed it to not be an obligation. If a Muslim missed a day, they could give charity to a poor person to make up the missed day of fasting. Again, the rule was relaxed to accommodate the pregnant, nursing mothers and elderly.

Imams say that fasting is for a fixed number of days, and if one of you are sick, or if one of you are on a journey, you will fast the same number of other days later on. For those who are capable of fasting (but still do not fast) there is a redemption: feeding a needy man for each day missed. Whoever voluntarily does more good than is required, will find it better for him; and that you should fast is better for you, if you only know (Surah Al Baqara 2:184).[10]

Muslims use fasting as a shield of protection from the evil spirits. It is compared to Jesus Christ's teaching in Matthew "But

---

[10] http://www.islamicstudies.info/tafheem.php?sura=2&verse=183&to=184

this kind never comes out except by prayer and fasting." (Matthew 17:21). All (except for those who have not yet reached puberty, any who are traveling, the elderly and infirm) are supposed to fast, as Ramadan is a holy month for Muslims. If women are menstruating, nursing or bleeding from childbirth, they are excused from fasting during that time, but are expected to make up their fasts so they do not sin. In this way, women are always falling in spiritual debt, falling behind in their requirements to be a Muslim. In the book "In the Land of Blue Burqas" by Kate McCord (2012), it is noted that elderly women sometimes fast into emaciation in order to make up a lifetime of missed fasts due to childbearing. Fasting for Muslims is to abstain from all things impure: lying, cheating, sexual desires, eating and drinking during the daylight hours. That means many Muslims eat copious amounts during the night - so you are actually exchanging daytime eating for night. It is terribly shameful for a Muslim to gain weight during Ramadan, but I personally have known people who have done that! If you think about it, they are usually asleep most of the day (especially women who are at home) and then are awake all night. In Saudi Arabia and other Muslim countries, businesses are allowed to close during the day and remain open at night. The weather is cooler, everyone eats, enjoys one another's company as they roam around the shops. We used to break our fast at parties and would host get-togethers in our home with friends who would visit over Ramadan. It was great fun to be awake at three in the morning, eating pizza, watching movies, playing cards and drinking tea. The whole house was awake and we would try to gorge ourselves until the last possible moment right before sunrise.

As I became older and lived in the United States, fasting during Ramadan was almost non-existent for me and my family. My parents worked during the day, while we went to school. There were tests, classes and to my horror, Physical Education (PE) classes. It was next to impossible for me to keep a fast during the day and exercise. I tried to keep a fast for a few days, especially in high school and college, but I would get horrible migraines. Since medical reasons were exempt, I thought this was a good loophole for me to escape from the fourth pillar's requirement - not really understanding that I had already been collecting a lifetime of sinful debt due to missed fasting days. In response to the question being posed to me, I told the pastor "Well, I've tried to fast, but I get headaches." He thought about it for a second and then crossed out the fasting line. He said "Nope - it is a requirement for all able bodied individuals to fast during Ramadan. Now let's take a look at the next."

The fifth pillar of Islam requires each and every Muslim to make the Pilgrimage to Mecca (Hajj). Finally, I was thankful about having one for sure. Between the first pillar (Shahada) and this last one, I had been on somewhat shaky ground. This one was easy, since there are only two answers: you made the pilgrimage or you did not. My parents were kind enough to have taken us on the pilgrimage to

Mecca when I was very young. I was old enough to have memories of this event but those memories are from a child's view and are further refreshed from family photos of us in Mecca during Hajj.

Hajj is the fifth pillar and is a sacred requirement for all Muslims. It is something that is performed in the last month of the Muslim calendar and pilgrims from all over the world, including people of all social standings attend (Quran -Al Hajj Surah 22 verse 27). It is not uncommon to see poor people walking alongside royalty. It is not just one day, but takes about five days to perform. There are several rituals that are an important part of Hajj, namely clothing, prayers, special restrictions, manner in which to perform Hajj and also a special way to indicate when a pilgrim has finished those requirements. Chapter 22 in the Quran, titled Al Hajj, states that all who are able should undertake the pilgrimage to the Kaaba in Mecca. You only have to perform this once in your lifetime, but there are many who make the pilgrimage more than once.

The Hadith promises great rewards for those who perform Hajj - when you return from the pilgrimage, all your sins are washed clean (Hadith 1521, Book of Hajj, Bukhari, Vol. 2). There are also different types of Hajj that can be performed with a litany of details and differences in the rites associated with each. There is Hajj-e-Tamattu, Hajj-e-Qiran and a special Hajj designated only for the residents of Mecca called Hajj-e-Ifrad.

I was very little at that time, but remember that our family had to plan the trip well in advance. My father was going to drive his car and we were all packed for the grand trip - grandparents, two daughters, mom and dad. There were a lot of preparations to make ahead of time because you cannot expect a store like Wal Mart to be there to take care of your needs. We had to purchase white Hajj clothes for all of us to wear. This is called "Ihram" in Arabic and it means "consecration" or to do something holy. It is a requirement as stated in the Hadith because the checklist for performing Hajj is not found in the Quran. My parents packed food, water, sandals for our feet and other safety items. All travelers are required by the government to limit the amount of money or valuables they bring. No jewelry, watches or accessories are allowed on women or men.

The moment you put on the Ihram (white clothes), you are then known as a "Muhrim" or one who performs the Hajj. There are boundaries designated by Mohammad around Mecca that delineate when you have entered into the holy land. Airplanes will announce this as they fly over so people will know and respect those guidelines[11]. For men, there is a two piece Ihram garment that is compulsory to wear. There is an unstitched white sheet that is wrapped around the waist (as a skirt) and another piece that goes around the body and over the shoulder. This is only a requirement for men. Women making the pilgrimage usually are dressed in a long white garment, with a white head cover. Women are not allowed to cover their face (the hijab or burqa veil is removed) nor can they wear gloves to cover their hands as some women do regularly in the

---

[11] http://www.quranandhadith.com/ihram/

middle east. As the pilgrims get ready for Hajj, it is recommended that they first bathe and trim body hair and nails, in order to groom themselves ahead of time before wearing Ihram. Supreme simplicity is key as women usually do not wear make-up or perfumes (not allowed to wear perfumes by the Hadith No. 833, Chapters on Hajj, Jami' At-Tirmidhi, Vol. 2; Hadith No. 2674). Once they are properly in the state of Ihram, they can offer prayer to Allah, announce their intention (called Niyyah in Arabic and Niyat in my language - Urdu) and then a Takbir (allahuakbar = God is Great) to begin Hajj and begin the walk down to the place of pilgrimage towards the Masjid al Haram. Just by omitting the Niyyah and Ihram, your Hajj would be declared invalid and you would not receive blessing because you did not perform the ritual correctly up to this point.

When you get to the Kaaba (Kaaba means cube = the black cube in the middle of Mecca), you can then begin what's called "Tawaf." It means to walk and circle the Kaaba counter clockwise seven times. You will see the term "circumambulation" noted for this activity - just means to walk around in a circle in a ceremonious manner. The Imams teach that the pattern of walking around the Kaaba is to mimic the planetary movements.

In the eastern-most corner of the Kaaba is a black stone, set in silver called the Hajar al aswad. Islamic tradition holds that it was a meteorite that had fallen from the sky and that Mohammad himself set it into the wall of the Kaaba around 629 AD. In addition, many believe that the Kaaba originally housed many pagan idols and also the black stone before Mohammad claimed the Kaaba for worship of Allah[12]. There is also another tradition that holds that Ibrahim (Abraham) built the original Kaaba as a shrine - there is a place near the Kaaba that is said to be Ibrahim's footprints, called the Station of Ibrahim. To start the Tawaf or walk, the pilgrim should start at a brown marble line on the floor and try to touch or kiss the black stone. There is a great deal of jostling that takes place at this point. As a small child, my dad put me upon his shoulders and allowed me to touch, feel and kiss the smooth black stone as he did. He also explained to me there that it was a touch that went back centuries and connected us to our prophet Mohammad. You then have to stop and start at certain places around the Kaaba and also recite prayer verses that indicate which round you are on[13].

After Tawaf, the pilgrim has to do Sa'ee (or "Sa'y") between the mountains of Safa and Marwa. This is located near the Kabaa and is an important part of the pilgrimage. You have to start at Safa and end at the Marwa by walking seven times to and from each location. This tradition may be fascinating to Christians and Jews alike. It comes from the time of Ibrahim and Hajar (called Hagar in the Bible). Tradition has it that when Ismail was born to Hajar, Ibrahim's first wife became jealous and threatened to kill her. Hajar wanted to run away but Ibrahim escorted her to the highest place in Mecca called "Zamzam." There were few people there at the time

---

[12] Khan Academy - https://www.khanacademy.org/humanities/art-islam/beginners-guide-islamic/a/the-kaaba
[13] http://www.dalil-alhaj.com/en/altawaf_mf_1.htm

and no system for transporting water.

After he left her, the water in the skins ran out. In the blistering desert sun, she and her nursing child became thirsty very quickly. She got up and ran to a mountain called Safa to climb up to see if she could

find someone to help them. In her panic and distress, she ran to the next mountain called Marwa. She ran back and forth seven times between the two mountains. She prayed that Allah would give her water and He answered her prayers by bringing forth water at Zamzam. There is a well that still gives water and they say if you drink from it, all your illnesses will be cured. There are separate places for men and women to drink.

In the Bible, Genesis 16 says that Hagar was sent to Arabia after Sarah (Abraham's wife) treated her harshly after she learned that she had conceived Abraham's child. She prayed to God in her distress and he answered her. The Bible says in Genesis 16:13 that "She gave this name to the LORD who spoke to her: "You are the God who sees me," for she said, "I have now seen the One who sees me (El Roi). The place where God spoke to her is called Beer-lahai-roi (translated as Well of the Living One[14]).

The Sa'ee was the worst part of the Hajj for me because you had to take your sandals off when you entered the area between Safa and Marwa. There was a dwarfed man who stood at attention and you gave him your shoes. There were hundreds of shoes there and the

---

[14] http://biblehub.com/commentaries/genesis/16-14.htm

man frightened me, for I had never seen anyone who looked quite like he did. Dropping off my sandals amid myriad of others added trauma to my fragile state. For rest of the pilgrimage, I was obsessed with the thought that someone was going to take my shoes. These are the things a young child thinks of - not the religious significance of the events that would be with me for a lifetime that my parents were telling me about, but concern over a dwarfed man who was looking after my sandals. I am sure at this point, we drank from the well at Zamzam, but I do not remember that.

After performing the Sa'ee ritual, men get their heads shaved and women can have their hair cut (they are not required to shave the head completely - only men). Hajj is almost done now. Pilgrims can go back to their hotel rooms and wait for the Day of Tarwiyah. In the morning, pilgrims set out for Mina in their Ihram and go there to pray. The next day, pilgrims go to Arafat in their Ihram. At sunset that day, the pilgrims go to another place called Muzdalifah then back to Mina. The next ritual is Yaum-e-Nahr (Day of Sacrifice)' –Dhul Hijj (The Day of Eid Al-Adha) in Jamarat, where there are three pillars, depicting Satan. Muslims have to throw stones at the largest pillar. This is then followed by the sacrifice of an animal. There are other days that remain that have pilgrims again stay in different locations, culminating in a final Tawaf al wida performed again at the Kaaba.

As in many aspects of Islam, there are different requirements for men and women. There is a website called Dalil-alhaj[15] that lists out some of the differences and how women are to behave during Hajj. In order to be concise, I have listed the sum of requirements for men and women during Hajj here:

Mandatory rites of Hajj
1. 'Ihram' and 'Niyyah'
2. Stay in Arafat (and not leaving till after sunset)
3. 'Tawaf-al-Ifadah'
4. Sa'ee

If anyone of these rites is missed or not done completely, the Hajj is invalid and incomplete.

After Sa'ee:
1. Stay in Mina
2. Stay in Muzdalifah
3. Stoning the Jamarat
4. Sacrificing an animal
5. 'Tawaf-al-wida'

There are so many days spent among hundreds of thousands of people in Mecca. The city overflows to the brim and hotels are usually booked months or even years in advance. It was almost impossible for my parents to get our car close to the location where

---

[15] http://www.dalil-alhaj.com/en/women.htm

we were staying. I remember vividly that there were many makeshift vendors with tented stalls doing business outside Mecca. It is not forbidden for business to take place or even profit to be made as long as people are not cheated while they are there for a sacred reason.

My mother and father allowed us to purchase souvenirs from our trip and yes, I did get my sandals back. It was an amazing journey - one that many never make. It was a trip worth remembering for all of us, especially once it fulfilled one of the sacred pillars of faith: Hajj.

The Decision

At this point, the pastor who was leading me through the Pillars of Faith looked at me and said "Three out of five pillars does not get a Muslim to Heaven." I knew immediately the shame of not praying five times a day or being able to fast through Ramadan. I knew that was my struggle daily and I felt the burden of trying to accomplish the religious requirements on my own. I was a terrible Muslim and terrible Muslims had to rely only on God's mercy to get to Heaven. Since all of Islam is based on works. The Quran specifically mentions the use of balance scales on Judgment Day (Qiyamat) in Surah 21:47 "And We will set up a just balance on the day of resurrection, so no soul shall be dealt with unjustly in the least; and though there be the weight of a grain of mustard seed, (yet) will We bring it, and sufficient are We to take account[16]." Muslims believe that there are two angels given to each believer called ""Kiraman Katibin" which translates to honorable recorders or noble writers[17]. One angel is placed upon your right shoulder and the other on the left shoulder. Five times a day, at the end of each prayer, Muslims say "Asalaam Alaykum Warahmatallah (May peace and mercy of Allah be upon you)." These two angels write down the good and bad deeds (Quran Surah 82:10-12) and do not miss one thing. Islamic tradition holds that the angel on the right is the nicer and more merciful of the two, since he writes the good deeds. The angel on the left will record all the bad things you do. The left side is associated with unclean things - an idea borrowed from Jewish traditions.

On Judgment Day, Qiyamat, each set of angels open their lists and present the accounts for their Muslim person. If the good deeds (thawaab in Arabic & sawaab in Urdu) outweigh the bad deeds (Ihthim in Arabic & gunnah in Urdu), then the Muslim goes to Paradise (Jannah). If the bad deeds outweigh the good then the Muslim goes to Hell or Jehannum. If you end up with equal good and bad deeds, most Muslims have no answer. Some will say that the Muslim enters into a state of limbo or being in between two

---

[16] https://www.al-islam.org/resurrection-maad-quran-ayatullah-ibrahim-amini/scale-deeds
[17] Hopler, Whitney
http://angels.about.com/od/AngelsReligiousTexts/a/Kiraman-Katibin-Muslim-Recording-Angels.htm

spiritual worlds. Others will say that they will implore Allah to be most merciful. Some will even say that their relatives will pray them into Heaven (there is a funeral prayer that takes place in many Muslim cultures where the deceased family will fervently pray their loved one into Paradise a belief based on Surah 59:10 from the Quran "And [there is a share for] those who came after them, saying, "Our Lord, forgive us and our brothers who preceded us in faith and put not in our hearts [any] resentment toward those who have believed. Our Lord, indeed You are Kind and Merciful".

Needless to say, all of this loomed over my head like a large cloud that day in the pastor's office. The knowledge of my own sinfulness, the sad state of my being a shoddy Muslim, and also knowing that Allah has an exacting standard for us on Judgment Day. If there was a list, my left angel's list was going to be much longer than the angel on the right shoulder. With that statement about not getting to Heaven still hanging in the air, I choked up and started sobbing into my hands.

The pastor laid a gentle hand on my shoulder and said "I asked you on Sunday why you came to church and you replied that you didn't know. I think you do know. So, I will ask you again... why did you come to church?" I answered candidly "Because God told me to." There was a look of victory and a big smile from the pastor. He said "YES! He did! Do you know why?" I shook my head to indicate I didn't know. I thought the message was for everyone except me. He said "Because God is giving you his grace."

I stopped crying at this point because I didn't understand. Grace is something that does not exist for Muslims. Everything is works. The deeds are what counts for you. If you mess up, that is a demerit that will be recorded for Judgment Day. Muslims are aware of this fact. There are even websites that tell Muslims how to increase their thawaab and tips on how to get their good deeds done quickly to increase the chances of getting to Paradise. Since only works existed and I had no concept of grace, I shook my head again to show that I didn't understand at all.

At this point, he did something unexpected. He looked around and on his desk was a bowl of wrapped chocolates. He placed one into the palm of his hand and extended it to me. He didn't say anything - he just presented the chocolate to me. I stared at him through my tears, looked at my husband who made a "mmmhummmm" sound and then back to the pastor. I said "Okay, you are handing a pregnant woman some chocolate." I took the chocolate, opened it up and popped it in my mouth. The pastor said "Are you enjoying it? How is it?" I replied "It's chocolate! It's good." He then said "That is grace."

Not having any spiritual understanding at all, I was so confused. "Chocolate is grace?" He replied "NO! Chocolate is not grace. Grace is unmerited, undeserved favor from God. You don't ask for it, He simply gives it out freely to all who will take it, accept it and enjoy it. You didn't ask me for the chocolate, yet I gave it to you. You took it and enjoyed it... that is grace from God."

The scales fell off my eyes in that instant. I did not know it yet, but that is what is said in Ephesians 2:8-10 "For it is by grace you have been saved through faith, and this not from yourselves; it is the gift of God, not by works, so that no one can boast. For we are God's workmanship, created in Christ Jesus to do good works, which God prepared in advance." Just as quickly the entire chapter in the Quran about Isa Masih that I could not reconcile with the life of Mohammad came to my mind. It made no sense until that moment.

I felt an enormous peace wash over me. I described it to my husband as wearing a terribly wrinkled shirt that doesn't sit comfortably - only to take a huge iron and take all those creases away. Every wrinkle had been smoothed out. All the tumblers fell into place and the locked door opened for me. It was overwhelming. I wanted to know... now what? The pastor said, well we should have you pray and confess that Jesus Christ is Lord. Do you confess that Jesus Christ is Lord and Savior, that he was raised from the dead and that he is the only way to Heaven? I said yes, I do and I am ready to pray. My husband, who had been quietly listening said "WHAT?"

All things pointed to Christ. In fact, it dawned on me about my husband's spiritual life. I was so surprised! I said "Stephen! Jesus Christ is the only thing that makes sense! This is why God wanted me to see who Christ is and why he kept telling me to go to church!" The pastor, caught up in the moment, agreed with me. He told me that it was the Holy Spirit who was telling me to go to church. His role in the trinity was to point to Christ. All things had been prepared beforehand by God so that I would walk in them! What a glorious truth to be revealed in one evening! My husband became emotional and said that God had been leading him towards Christ as well but since I was studying the Quran so much, he was afraid of how that would drive our marriage apart.

In the church office that evening, we both bowed our heads, confessed, prayed and accepted Christ at the same time as our Lord and Savior. Our family of five was baptized on January 28, 2007.

Chapter 8

Disowned Again

After our family's baptism, we were quickly initiated to what it was like to go to church on a regular basis but more importantly, what a Christian family looked like. We started our Christian education by reading the Bible and attending Bible Study classes -- all of them! We were both hungry for God's word and had no time to lose. At this time, we realized that the pastor who met with me on that Friday after VBS was an interim pastor. The church had been looking for a senior pastor for almost three years. In March, there was a congregational meeting (our first ever) and so we attended because the Pastor Search Committee had found someone. They played a brief video of a man preaching from the pulpit and then announced his name. I looked at my husband and said "I think that's an Arabic name?" I was confused because the man on the video did not fit my own assumption and experience of what Arabs looked like, since he had a fair complexion with light eyes. As the committee further related to the congregation, they said that new head pastor was from Syria, a former Muslim who was raised in Saudi Arabia and had accepted Christ in college. He had been disowned by his father and paid a big price for his conversion.

I fell to my knees. I had been praying for God to help me with this and also for telling my parents. I did not want to tell them. In fact, I was coming up with all kinds of excuses for not telling them... things were just better left the way they were.

Our new head pastor started during the summer and we invited his family to come to our home for dinner. He asked me about my conversion and naturally, how my parents were taking it. I honestly told him that I didn't believe they needed to know. He thoughtfully considered this and after a few minutes of not speaking, he said "That's a beautiful cross necklace you are wearing." I thanked him and then he said "Would you wear that in front of your parents and family?" I felt deflated. Deflated and scared at the same time. Jesus says in the Gospel of Matthew 5:15-16 "Nor do people light a lamp and put it under a basket, but on a stand, and it gives light to all in the house. In the same way, let your light shine before others, so that they may see your good works and give glory to your Father who is in heaven."

When I heard that verse, I knew that was what I was supposed to do. It was wrong for me to keep the Gospel to myself and not share it with my family who had not heard. This was Good News - that Christ did the work, took the punishment for your sin and gave you eternal life. Why would a Christian keep this to themselves?

Later on in my ministry to others who converted from Islam, I found that many who accept Christ as their Lord and Savior do not want to share immediately with their families. A foreign exchange student from Senegal at our local University told me that he would lose all his inheritance as his dad would disown him if he chose to be a Christian. He would not be allowed back to his village, their home and his family would cut him off. He said this would not be something he would want to do - to share the news of Christ with his family.

Another woman from Uzbekistan had converted to Christianity from Islam over a year ago before I met her. She told me tearfully that she had to hide this decision from her husband because he would take away her children. Over the next two years, she decided she could not hide this anymore and she told him. What followed afterwards was a terrible chain of events - from her family locking her in their home when she came to visit them in another State with her children. They took her children away, gave them to her husband and then the family threatened her. This was here in the United States. People find it hard to believe that this kind of persecution exists in this nation. She called on her family in Christ who were able to give her money and a ticket to come back to her home. She was finally able to reconcile with her husband, but he is not yet a believer. Even though she lives in a Muslim home, she is glad she no longer has to hide her faith and believes that through prayer her husband will come to believe in Christ as well.

After spending time in deep prayer, I decided to tell my parents. I had "Been there, done that" before in the turmoil I had faced when I had decided to marry an American. Until that moment of decision, I had not realized that God had prepared me many years ago for the ultimate test of my faith. To be disowned once was fine, but I had not abdicated Islam back then. Now, to turn my back on Islam meant to turn my back on so much of what I knew. I wrote a letter to my parents and after I mailed it, I also picked up the phone to tell them. I felt so scared and anxious. Before anyone picked up the phone, I felt overcome with peace and felt The Lord tell me "Don't worry about him. He is your earthly father. I am your true Heavenly Father. You are doing this for me." My father answered.

The love I have for my dad surpasses many things. He was the one I had looked up to for all my life. I desired to emulate him and how he worked. I loved his sense of humor and the way others were always drawn to him. He is such a charismatic person with a ready smile. But not for me - not this time. The anger I heard in his voice was unforgettable. The first time I was disowned due to my marriage, he did not talk to me. The delivery of the news had been delegated to my older sister who was the spokesperson for the family. This time, however, my father told me directly that the disowning was for real. There would be no return. I had no inheritance or family and he had only two daughters. For him, I had died that day.

An Act of Mercy

When I share that I was disowned by my family with others in the United States, people are aghast! How could someone do that to their children? How could that be in the 21st century in the United States? Why would someone do that to a child they loved?

What they don't understand is that to the outsiders, being disowned may look cruel, but I believe it is an act of mercy. In the Quran (2:217), an apostate (one who has turned their back to Islam and converted to another religion) has the penalty of death on their head for men. For women, it is life imprisonment. The website Al Islam[18] clearly states this chilling reality in this way:

The punishment prescribed by the shari`ah for apostasy is death. Even the terms used by the shari`ah for apostates give the idea of treason to this whole phenomenon. "Murtad" means apostate. Murtad can be of two types: fitri and milli.

(1) "Murtad Fitri" means a person who is born of a Muslim parent and then he rejects Islam.

"Fitrah" means creation. The term "murtad fitri" implies that the person has apostate from the faith in which he was born.

(2) "Murtad Milli" means a person who converted to Islam and then later on he rejects Islam. Milli is from millat which means religion. The term "murtad milli" implies that the person has become an apostate from his religion and the Muslim community.

---

[18] https://www.al-islam.org/articles/apostasy-islam-sayyid-muhammad-rizvi

In the first case, the apostasy is like the treason against God; whereas in the second case, the apostasy is like the treason against the Muslim community. Probably, that is why the Sh`iah jurisprudence deals with these two kinds of murtads differently:

A former kāfir (apostate) who became a Muslim and then apostates (murtad milli), he is given a second chance: if he repents, then he is not to be killed; but if he does not repent, then he is to be killed. But one who is born as a Muslim and then apostates (murtad fitri), he is to be killed even if he repents. It is important to understand that in case a murtad fitri repents, Allāh may accept his repentance and he may be forgiven in the hereafter, but he still has to go through the punishment prescribed for his treason in this world (for a detailed discussion on the acceptance of the repentance (tawba) by a murtad fitri, see the transcript of the late Ayatullāh al-Khu'ā's lectures by Shaykh al-Gharawi, at-Tanqāh, vol. 3, p. 224-229.).

This punishment is only applicable in case of apostasy by men; in case of women, the punishment is not death but life imprisonment. And if such a woman repents, then her repentance is accepted and the punishment is lifted.

Even though the commentaries say that others may misinterpret the language (since Muslims believe that the Arabic should not be translated to another language due to mistakes man would make to decipher what God is saying). An interesting thing to note here is that while the Quran does not say clearly that death is the consequence, the Hadith (traditional writings that are the basis for understanding the writings in the Quran), is much clearer. Sahih Bukhari is the main place many Muslims go to see what the traditions uphold:

Bukhari, Volume 9, Book 83, Number 17[19]
Narrated Abdullah: "Allah's Messenger said, "The blood of a Muslim who confesses that none has the right to be worshipped but Allah and that I am His Messenger, cannot be shed except in three cases: in Qisas (equality in punishment) for murder, a married person who commits illegal sexual intercourse and the one who reverts from Islam (Apostate) and leaves the Muslims."

Bukhari, Volume 9, Book 84, Number 57[20]
Narrated 'Ikrima, "Some atheists were brought to Ali and he burnt them. The news of this event, reached Ibn Abbas who said, "If I had been in his place, I would not have burnt them, as Allah's messenger forbade it, saying, "Do not punish anybody with Allah's punishment (fire)." I would have killed them according to the statement of Allah's Messenger, "Whoever changed his Islamic religion, then kill him."

---

[19] http://www.usc.edu/org/cmje/religious-texts/hadith/bukhari/083-sbt.php

[20] http://www.usc.edu/org/cmje/religious-texts/hadith/bukhari/084-sbt.php

Bukhari, Volume 9, Book 84, Number 58[21]

Narrated Abu Burda: "Abu Musa said... Behold there was a fettered man beside Abu Musa. Muadh asked, "Who is this (man)?" Abu

Musa said, "He was a Jew and became a Muslim and then reverted back to Judaism." Then Abu Musa requested Muadh to sit down but Muadh said, "I will not sit down till he has been killed. This is the judgment of Allah and his messenger," and repeated it thrice. Then Abu Musa ordered that the man be killed, and he was killed. Abu Musa added, "Then we discussed the night prayers..."

The Hadith does not differentiate between men or women. It explicitly states "whoever" and when added to the many laws that the major Sunni Jurists (Mujtahids) uphold, there is no question that killing an apostate is upheld as a part of the Islamic Holy War or Jihad. When taken in light of all these jurisdictions around the denunciation of Islam by someone who was born into a Muslim family where both parents are Muslim, the penalty is a steep one to pay. The way a Muslim family can uphold their honor in a Muslim community (Ummah) is to disown their child. It shows the others that they know and understand the teachings and also what is expected. In the West, disowning is the right thing to do.

---

[21] http://www.usc.edu/org/cmje/religious-texts/hadith/bukhari/084-sbt.php

I personally believe being disowned to be an act of mercy for this reason: my father took a stance and told the Muslim community that he was doing right by his family. He could not and would not accept this behavior and that he was, to put it into American terms "Taking care of business" in his own home. They did not need to worry about their daughter corrupting or polluting the community. She did not exist.

The phone call ended with me telling my father that I loved him and that I would pray that one day we would be reconciled. He sadly told me that would not happen and that he did not need or want my prayers. It was a terrible burden to bear.

The pain of separation is difficult for both sides. Many in the United States don't understand that for a Muslim person, apostasy to Islam and conversion to Christianity can exact a huge price, including one's life. There is a cost to following Jesus. In Luke 14:25-30, Jesus speaks about this plainly:

Large crowds were now traveling with Jesus, and He turned and said to them, "If anyone comes to Me and does not hate his father and mother and wife and children and brothers and sisters — yes, even his own life—he cannot be My disciple. And whoever does not carry his cross and follow Me cannot be My disciple. Which of you, wishing to build a tower, does not first sit down and count the cost to see if he has the resources to complete it? Otherwise, if he lays the foundation and is unable to finish the work, everyone who sees it will ridicule him, saying, 'This man could not finish what he started to build.'

Giving up your family and your old life is a part of the cost of according to this passage. Renouncing all things seems to be the trend for those who follow Jesus, yet who understands it in the United States? For the Muslim, there are no cultural or geographic boundaries. The cost comes whether you are in the United States, in the Middle East or anywhere else in the world. The only difference is that for a Muslim to turn his back on Islam in a Muslim country is the same as signing a death warrant. At least in the United States there can be some sort of security for some, but not all.

Chapter 9

Our Father - The Power of Prayer

The cost of following Christ is recounted many times in the Bible. The Apostles themselves left everything to follow Him who was the Way, the Truth and the Life. Peter didn't look back to his fishing nets and Nathaniel got up right away from his reading and meditations under the fig tree. Each of them died for their Lord and Savior Jesus. So why does it seem like such a high price to pay for us today?

When I share my testimony with others I am inevitably asked if I am fearful that someone might come and kill me when they find out that I converted. The answer I give is that everyone has to die. Death is a part of the equation here on earth. Those who are born have to die - there's no way around it. Either you die of natural causes or unnatural ones. For me, the way I can glorify Christ is by dying in service to Him. That is the truth. I am not trying to embellish it or make myself out to be more than what I am. I have shared this truth with my children and they know that I am not afraid, for as the Apostle Paul put it in Philippians 1:21, "For me, to live is Christ, and to die is gain."

There is a great comfort in knowing that you belong completely to God. That you don't just have to complete a checklist for him daily and then live in fear of the balance scales of God's judgment. There is comfort and joy that comes from knowing that you cannot pay the price of sin, that there is ONLY ONE who can and has done that already for you - even if you were the only one in need of His mercy, that Jesus Christ would have gone to his death on the Cross just for you. What an amazing truth that is to live by! How free am I now to look for ways that I could share that truth with others. The only problem was that those whom I loved the most had shut the door on my existence.

After my conversation with my father, the next thing I went to was prayer. I went to my knees and prayed fervently for restoration and for my parents to open their ears, hearts and minds to the truth God had revealed to me through Christ Jesus. In Matthew 7:7, Christ tells us to ask and we will receive, seek and we shall find, and knock for the door will be opened. This is the promise I went to at my time of abandonment. I knew that all was stripped away and that prayer was still my greatest spiritual weapon. I asked every single Christian group I spoke to and belonged to for prayer in this effort. In Ephesians 6, the Armor of God is one of the most well known and loved picture in scripture. I learned through attending Bible Study Fellowship that every single weapon in the Armor is defensive, except for prayer and the sword of the Spirit which is the word of the Lord. Paul says in Ephesians 6:18 "And pray in the Spirit on all occasions with all kinds of prayers and requests. With this in mind, be alert and always keep on praying for all the Lord's people." I prayed in earnest for reconciliation and for the Lord to open a way into my parents' lives. After a year and a half, the Lord did just that and more.

One day unexpectedly, my mother called and said she wanted to see our baby, Sarah and the boys. The call seemed very tentative on her part, but I was overjoyed at her reaching out to me. She set the ground rules clearly and the guidelines sounded like the Military's "Don't Ask, Don't Tell" policy: Don't talk about Jesus or even mention his name or anything about Christianity and they wouldn't ask me to recant my conversion. I agreed to this demand. I had the blessing of reading a quote attributed to St. Francis of Assisi that says "Preach the Gospel at all times, and if necessary use words." This was what I held onto as I reached across to accept this olive branch that was extended to me. I have mentioned before that my mother is a peacemaker. I pray the verse from Matthew 5:9 "Blessed are the peacemakers, for they will be called children of God" for her. I pray that because the Lord has given her this ability to make peace (not just in our immediate family, but also in her extended family and friends), that He will and call her to Him one day so she can find peace for her soul.

Another specification that was requested was that only the children and I should come (excluding my husband). I believe the reason for this was that they still blamed him as a Christian for my conversion - not knowing that the Lord compelled me to come and He brought our entire family along to kneel before Him.

When I told him that I was asked to come, that a deal had been struck, and that I wasn't even sure if I was staying at my parent's home (I really was not sure if my dad was on board or if this was just my mom making this invitation without his knowledge or approval). My discerning husband told me that he felt at great unease over all of this! For me to travel to California with three children ten and under, to not be sure if anyone would come to the airport, to not be sure where we would stay, to not be sure if an angry friend of the family would do me physical harm... the list of fears went on and on. He was not going to let his beloved bride go and do all that by herself.

I had not thought about the reality of any of those things. I simply was ecstatic that the Lord had heard my prayers and that this would be a first step towards reconciliation. Since this was a complicated matter, I asked all of my Bible Study groups (there were several of them at the time!) to commit themselves to prayer for me and my family members. We also sought counsel with our head pastor, who greeted the news with joy. He reiterated that while there may be danger and a fear of the unknown, that this was something

\

that God had arranged and that we should rejoice at the opportunity to go. Thus, it was decided that the children and I would go across the United States into the unknown and fight spiritual battles unseen.

The power of prayer cannot be underestimated. About a week before the children and I were to depart, we heard at church that a missionary family had recently decided to relocate from overseas back to the United States. They were a husband and wife team of physicians who had been ministering to Muslims in several countries and they moved about two weeks prior to the announcement to a location that was maybe one to two miles away from my parents home! Can you believe that? I knew that was the hand of God.

One of the main concerns Stephen had was that most of our network was either Muslim family members or other friends who were about an hour and a half away. In the case of an emergency or if I needed help, no one could get to me quickly. Here, the Lord provided a family that was associated with our church and had a heart for reaching Muslims for Christ Jesus. I got their number and contact information and called them saying "You don't know me, but the Lord knows I needed you right now." They were thrilled that I would reach out to them with this request and we exchanged contact information, addresses and also set up a time where we could possibly meet for lunch near my parents' home. Again, it turned out that the wife worked at a hospital about five miles from my parents' home. This was the second confirmation I received that this was something to rejoice about and that the Lord had already gone before me. This was the same as Hagar when she saw her prayers being answered in the Arabian desert - He truly is El Roi, God who sees me.

The time for the long-awaited trip arrived. We had decided not to depend upon anyone for a ride, so I had reserved a minivan and drove to my parents' home from the airport, all the while praying and listening to worship music. I brought along some songs that were already favorites and these songs helped to not just calm me but also put me in the right frame of mind. I would be lying if I said I was not anxious. I was not sure what to expect. Would my children go inside and I would be turned away at the door? What if this was something that was planned by someone else without the love that my parents had for me - what if this was a devious plan and a trap set for me? I prayed for God to take away my fears, for He does not give us a Spirit of fear, but of power and love and self-control (2 Timothy 1:7). This was my truth and it was the rock upon which I would stand. My husband's sister shared a beautiful verse with me that I had also memorized "So we can confidently say, 'The Lord is my helper; I will not fear; what can man do to me?'" from Hebrews 13:6. Do we really believe this in our everyday lives? I will attest to the fact that it was not until that trip that I learned to believe this verse was absolutely true. We, who have been given the Spirit of God to indwell us, travel daily with a Mighty God. If we believe this to be true, then I think our lives as Christians would look dramatically different! By the time I reached their home (it's an hour and a half drive from the airport), I felt I had truly been fortified in prayer. I felt more reassured and confident in what God was doing. There was most definitely a supernatural plan at work and I had been invited to participate in seeing what God would do.

As I entered their home, there is a small alcove adorned with a mirror and a marble entry table. The table had a new figurine I had never seen - it was a lion, seated with a lamb. Tears sprang up to my eyes and I got a knot in my throat. I knew that El Roi was there. I took a deep breath and asked my mother about it right then and there - what was this marvelous scene (I was sure she didn't understand the Biblical meaning), where did she get it and why did she get it? The answer was no less miraculous. She smiled and said "It's amazing, isn't it? Well, I saw it in a gift shop that I don't normally go to. I needed a present for someone at work so I decided to stop in to find something. I saw this figure at the front. It was so strange and I was captivated by it. I looked at the price and it was much more than what I wanted to spend that day, so I bought the gift I came for and went home. A few days after, I kept thinking about that Lion statue. It was the end of the week and I thought that they probably wouldn't have it there anyway. There was only one and I was sure it had been sold by now, for it truly was extraordinary. I had extra time at lunch, so I went back to the store. They still had it, but someone had asked to place it on hold. They contacted the person and they didn't answer or didn't want it... so, I can't believe I got it!"

One of the most difficult things about that story was that I had to keep my mouth shut. I couldn't tell my mom that the Lion was the Lion of Judah and the lamb was the unblemished Lamb of God, Christ Jesus. I couldn't tell her that seeing the figure at the entrance of her house brought me peace and further confirmation that this was God's plan. I couldn't tell her any of these things, so I had to tell her simply that yes, I agreed. The art was indeed extraordinary and that the scene was truly captivating and moving. In Isaiah 11:6, there is a passage that says "The wolf will live with the lamb, the leopard will lie down with the goat, the calf and the lion and the yearling together; and a little child will lead them." Jesus Christ, our shepherd leads us into a life of peace and He takes away our fears. This doesn't mean that all things are going to go great and that you will lead a life of luxury. It simply means that He walks with you when you walk in obedience to Him. My life had taken a new course with Christ as my shepherd. I know he was leading me into peace and walking me through the valley of darkness that day as I entered their home.

The visit was awkward at best. My mother tried to make everything as comfortable as she could possibly make it, given the circumstances. I was allowed to stay at their home, in fact, my mom gave us the largest room so the children could sleep there with me. She was so happy and overjoyed to see the little ones and she showered them with gifts. For my dad, I believe the visit was forced upon him. He had a disconnected presence that could seem a bit strained at times. When I would walk into a room, he would walk out. I happened to walk into the dining room when he had been eating a meal and he left his plate at the table so that he didn't have to sit with me. That was a sad situation and was emotionally difficult for me, but I knew that forcing him would end up harming our fragile threads of reconciliation. So, I simply walked out of the room and tried to respect his space. He was his sweet self with the children and they were able to laugh, joke and spend time with both of my parents for the remainder of the visit.

Sometimes we think that God has sent only us into a particular situation or that we are somehow responsible for sharing the Gospel and making everyone see. While this is not an excuse for refusing to share the Gospel when you are called to do so, I believe it is a limited view of how God uses others in our family to witness. Jacob was almost ten years old and Joshua was almost eight years old at the time of the visit. Sarah was about a year and a half. The boys liked to be fairly independent and since I was so preoccupied with the trip, I had asked each of them to pack their own suitcase. I didn't know what they had packed (I made sure they at least had underwear & socks) until we got to California. Each day, our middle son Joshua wore a t-shirt from our church's Wednesday night program, Vacation Bible School or any other shirt with the name "Jesus" or a cross on it. I did not ask him to do any of this. We had, however, discussed that their grandparents did not believe in Jesus

Christ as we did and also that we had to approach them respectfully. I did not mention that I was not allowed to talk about Jesus - my husband and I had decided that the mandate was for me and not for the kids. The Lord could use them as He wished. The Holy Spirit uses the least of these to make His mission known. He points all to Christ Jesus and many times, He will use the little ones to do so.

Another thing that brought me peace was to know that even though my husband was not with me, Jesus says that wherever two or more are gathered in His name, there He is also with them (Matthew 18:19-20). My children were there with me. We prayed in the car together, we prayed in the morning and each night. We prayed over our meals. We prayed in all things and at all times. To see their sweet heads bent over in prayer with their small hands joined together with me is an image that is hard to forget. The peace that passes all understanding came in a flood during that time. It is true, when we are pushed to our limits as Christians in what we believe and what we do not believe is when we meet face to face with those whom we hold most dear to our heart. My parents have always loved me and I have loved them, but the love that Christ Jesus has put into my heart for them is a true love... one that is not born out of obligation to them for anything they can do for me. It is a love that He gives me that allows me to see them through His eyes.

The true test for me came when He asked me to forsake all others for His kingdom. The forsaking in this case was done by my parents due to their obligations and beliefs. For me, gaining Christ and the assurance of life eternal the minute you confess with your mouth that Christ is Lord was amazing. That was a precious gift given to me by God that I could not give up for anything or anyone - no matter how deeply I loved them. When God gives, He doesn't just give us things in a miserly fashion. The gifts we receive from Him outweigh all others. They come in the form of assurance of salvation, in peace of mind and in rest for our wandering soul.

Chapter 10

Baptisms

The year of our commitment to Christ brought about profound changes in our individual lives, in our family and also extended family. I was not the only one the Lord has influenced in this journey. My husband's testimony to his side of the family was an astounding thing to consider. He has been a leader in the way others see his strength and seriousness of pursuit. His family was a part of our baptism and we had a chance to share with them our decision to follow Christ.

My husband's grandparents were Christian and they modeled Christ to my husband as he spent his childhood summers with them in Wyoming. They were the first people we called after we accepted Christ as our Lord and Savior. One of the sweetest memories I have is of my getting on the phone with his grandmother, Estelle. Beaming from ear to ear, I told her excitedly "Grandma, I am a Christian now! I accepted Christ!" I could hear the joy and almost see her smile through the telephone line when she chuckled and said "Sweetheart, in my heart, I have always known you were a

Christian!" She was not surprised and recognized the signs of how The Lord had been working in my life even before I had seen them. She knew about my love for sewing and I had shared with her years earlier that when a local Methodist Church that had a Mother's Day Out (kind of a daytime or a babysitting program) and needed volunteers to help sew cloth nativity sets for their children, that only one person showed up... a Pakistani Muslim woman. I had not shared with that church that I was Muslim. Joshua was around three or four years old and had attended their Mother's Day Out program. When I look back, I see that was during the time after 9/11 when God had been calling out to me. I spent hours sewing six nativity sets and hand-embroidering them with gold thread and small seed beads. The irony and humor of that situation is still with me. God already had me in His sight and I never even knew it.

After our family was baptized in 2007, my husband's sister and her two sons were baptized the following year. The year after that, my husband's younger brother and his two sons were baptized. Stephen's parents were baptized when they were younger and are now involved in a church they attend.

In 2014, something amazing happened while I was visiting my parents. One evening after the dishes had been cleared away from dinner, my father and I were the only ones left at the table. We like to sit and talk about things - from poetry (my dad has thousands of lines memorized, from Urdu poets to British ones), to literature and other things. There was a pause in our conversation and I could sense that he was getting ready to ask me something that might rub me the wrong way or would be awkward. I try to be in prayer at all times, seeking the Holy Spirit's wisdom and choice of words. So, I quickly said a small prayer in my heart "Lord, whatever it is, please keep my words blanketed in love." To my absolute surprise, my dad said "There are a few things I have been thinking about and wanted to ask you. Can you tell me what the word 'Denomination' means?" Seriously, I almost fell out of my chair. I was only hoping that my facial expressions were not reflective of the way I felt inside. My heart started pounding. I could not believe that my dad was the one who wanted to breach the "Don't Ask, Don't Tell" rule that was instituted years ago.

I took a deep breath and smiled. I said that it had been very confusing to me what Baptist, Presbyterian, Methodist had to do with following Christ. I told him that when we joined the church, that we were given a book called "How to spell Presbyterian" by James Angell because many who called themselves Christian did not understand the basic tenets of their denomination. The bottom line was that while all believed in the divinity of Christ, there were differences in the way they saw certain teaching. For example, on the issue of Baptism: Methodists and Presbyterians sprinkled while the Baptists believed in full immersion under water.

His Engineering mind was computing that information and lining it up with his facts. I could see the working of his thoughts, except that my answer brought about another question from my dad. This one floored me even more than the first question. He asked "What is Baptism and why do Christians do it?" If I had a quick pulse over the first question, this second question brought about heart palpitations! I was beside myself. What a great question to ask! This was more thought about Christianity than I had given it before I had converted. To be honest, I had not ever considered what Baptism was nor how it applied to me. Now, to have my father asking about the significance of the process was like a dream come true.

I tried to calmly (so I wouldn't jump for joy right in the middle of our discussion) explain that Baptism was something that had been practiced from before Jesus' time. I told him that the Jews performed Baptism as an outward sign of spiritual cleansing. John the Baptist was baptizing people to repent and prepare the way of the Lord before Jesus started his ministry (John 1:23). The way it was explained to me at my conversion was that Baptism is not a requirement for salvation. It is a sacrament (something holy and set apart for God's purpose) that Jesus himself did and that it denotes an outward sign of an inner truth. Baptism was an outward sign of dying to yourself, repenting of sins, and coming out of the water as a new creation. It was symbolic of death and rebirth and it publicly demonstrated when a new Christian joined a community of believers (1 Corinthians 12:13).

Later on, I came to understand that Christ had also commanded Baptism in the Great Commission in Matthew 28: 19-20 "Go and make disciples of all nations, baptizing them in the name of the Father and of the Son and of the Holy Spirit, and teaching them to obey everything I have commanded you. And surely I am with you always, to the very end of the age." Baptism is truly one of the ways we identify with Christ in the way he has redeemed us. It was interesting to follow my dad's line of questioning about Baptism. I finally got the nerve up to ask him "Why did you want to know?" He told me simply that he had always been curious about it. I knew I was to leave it at that.

That night, I went to bed with a heart filled with gladness. I knew that God had been working in my father's heart and I prayed fervently for that brilliant intellectual curiosity to get the better of him. I prayed for God to inspire him to spend more and more time on the internet looking for answers that would lead him directly to Christ Jesus.

Little did I know that night that God's plan had been unfolding for a couple of years. I did not know that the following year (in 2015), my parents and I would attend a Baptism together! My parents and my sisters, along with their families came to join us as we celebrated our oldest son, Jacob's High School graduation. Close friends of ours attended a party at my parents' home in California a couple of years prior. They knew my family would be in Oklahoma for graduation and they gently inquired if all of us would be interested in attending the Baptism of their son. The Baptism was a special request from their son to be done by immersion in their backyard pool. Deep down, I knew this may have been something that God had set into motion - if nothing else, to help satisfy my father's curiosity. After discussion with my husband, the son's father went to my dad and respectfully asked if they would consider attending his son's Baptism, which would be followed by a party to celebrate. My dad graciously accepted the invitation!

There were also other opportunities through the years to witness to the rest of my family, including praying for my older sister and giving her a Bible. My sisters are not practicing Islam in any way, shape or form. They hold to the cultural aspect of it only and do the things that are pleasing to my parents and to put on a facade for the community. They have both made it painfully clear to me how they feel about my acceptance of Christianity and also how vocal I am about professing my faith and sharing the testimony God has given me. It is deeply offensive to them that I write a blog about my past and bring my family into it. I was asked by both of them personally to cease and desist. My older sister actually confirmed me in my conviction to share the Gospel by telling me that "it seems like you don't care for your family. You are always putting God first and our family second." I corrected her by saying "Thank you for noticing that I put God first. That is where He belongs. He is first and foremost in my life. He is the only one to whom I owe allegiance. In fact, I owe Him everything. Second place belongs to my husband. My children come third and you come a distant fourth." That was probably not the most loving answer to her frustration and anger with me, but it was the truth. I praised God that she had noticed that my blog writings pointed to God first and God alone.

There are times that I have come into direct conflict with my family about my relationship with Christ. Out of consideration for them, I will not go into further detail here. There are many families who have stories similar to mine. There is a distinct and costly price you pay when you accept Christ Jesus as your Lord and Savior and then forsake all others for Him. He never promised us that it would be easy. In fact, He said in John 15:18 that "If the world hates you, know that it has hated me before it hated you." When I share my testimony with others, a point I try to emphasize is that when I held a Muslim world view, I had many assumptions, fears and stereotypes about Christians. Now, as a Christian, the Lord has equipped me to address commonly held beliefs, fears and stereotypes Christians have about Muslims. Some people have confessed to me that they were ashamed of being terrified of Muslims and that both my background and testimony have helped them to understand the other side. The media can give us a skewed view of both sides and can cause us to have an unconscious bias.

I am still in awe of how God has been working in our family's life. Author and Christian apologist Ravi Zacharias (2007) wrote a book called "The Grand Weaver." In it, he shares a poignant story of seeing the cloth makers in India weave together intricate designs for their Sari fabric. In India, the main cloth weaver is usually the father of the family and the tradition is passed down generation to generation. Over the course of many years, the father patiently shows his son, the apprentice, how to change color quickly in the cloth. As the son sits on the floor with a basket of multicolored threads in his hand, he is physically unable to see what the father is seeing and doing above his head. All he knows is that at pertinent times, the father directs him to hand him the specific color of thread he needs at a particular part of the process.

The illustration is beautiful description to show the beauty of God working in our life. He sits above, looking at the full tapestry and intricate design. Only He knows how He has woven these threads together. He can see the beginning of the design and knows how it will look at the end. I may not know what He has planned for tomorrow, the next day or for the future, but I do know that I am confident that His hand is upon our family and that He is very interested in the details and is at work through His Holy Spirit.

Chapter 11

Of Love & Legacy

When I was a child, I used to speak like a child, think like a child, reason like a child; when I became a man, I did away with childish things. For now we see in a mirror dimly, but then face to face; now I know in part, but then I will know fully just as I also have been fully known. But now faith, hope, love, abide these three; but the greatest of these is love.

~ 1 Corinthians 3:11-13

When I was a Muslim, the only thing I knew was that religion was a series of steps you took to become closer to God. I believed that by following the prescribed steps, you could earn your way into Heaven. I did not understand that Christianity was not just another religion, but was a love relationship. Those who are of the Eastern mindset will undoubtedly roll their eyes at this statement, for love is something that you only find in the movies.

For everything else, there is a contract and an expressed give and take that occurs. Seeing the world through that lens gave me permission to be very selfish. It was all about me - I could take the steps, I could work my way and I could decide how and when I wanted to engage into any type of relationship. I chose only those who could do something for me.

One day when I was teaching a course on how to evangelize to Muslims, an elderly gentleman smiled about how passionate I was about reaching others and said aloud that he was curious about how I was before I met Christ. Since my husband was in the classroom, I asked him to address that question to him. I felt like he could and would give him an honest response. Everyone laughed because they thought I was putting my husband on the spot to say something nice about me. But, my husband knew that I wanted to share the absolute truth. He shared with the class the truth about me - that I was driven. I was intensely focused on the wrong things with an intensity. I wanted a career (which I had at the Campbell Soup Company), I wanted a family (we had two children at the time), I wanted it all. I was willing to pay any price for financial gain and wanted to be in control of all things. I was competitive, to a fault, and was in competition even with my own husband's career. I wanted more, bigger, better, faster. This drive resulted in my being fairly combative when things didn't go my way. This caused friction and a rift between my parents.

Not only was religion a source of frustration for me, but the energy that I poured into worldly gains in order to please myself and have it all was something that I tried to hide behind a mask of being a workaholic. We lived in California at that time and I was on the path to success. I put all of my energy into taking care of everything except my family (parents included). I simply didn't have time for any of them.

I have mentioned before that my relationship with my parents was childish. I wanted, wanted, wanted and when motives or other ideas were questioned by them, I would get mad. The relationship was based on what my parents could do for me. They did do a lot for me, particularly financially and I was willing to lie to them to keep the peace. This was the pattern since I could remember. You want something, you ask your parents, then you lie in order to justify it or get it and that is the end of the story. It was not a healthy relationship nor was it based on purity of love or intention. If you would have asked me at that time how my relationship was with my parents, I would have said that it was fine. It was not fine and it had not been fine for a very long time. I saw them as champions of an antiquated culture and as enforcers of religious rules. These were rules that got in the way of what I wanted. The ironic thing is that I knew it was wrong. I knew it was wrong to behave in that way, to lie and get your own way. It was something that ate at my conscience.

Accepting Christ brought about a change in all aspects of my life. We had a pastor who once told us to tell those who were contemplating Christianity that if they liked their life the way it was, not to read the Bible. It is the living word of God and it breathes life into every aspect of your being. It will bring about changes in all things if you acknowledge it as truth.

I began to pray for God to give me Christ's eyes to see. Every time I spoke to my mother, we would end up arguing. I would own my opinion and tell her she was wrong. My anger was barely below the surface. I began to not only pray to see my mom the way Christ would saw her, but I also started the practice of praying when I saw the phone call was from my mom. Slowly, I started to see not only the poor way in which I had been treating my mom but also the huge amount of blame I had placed squarely on her shoulders. Basically I had blamed her for all the bad things in our family and gave the praises to my dad. On the positive side, I began to see the strong values and work ethic my parents had instilled in me.

I am truly my mother's child. All this time, I had been so blind that I could not see that I was trying to argue with myself and blame it on my mother. My mom is absolutely brilliant, a progressive, highly-educated woman on the cutting edge of society. She is brave and fearless. She blazed a path by going to medical school in a third world country when the men in her city were against education for women. She became a professional who was given accolades in Saudi Arabia as an OBGYN. Female physicians are still a rarity there. She is a peace maker and she is blessed for doing that in our family. These are things that still bring tears to my eyes when I think about how unfair I have been to her. I had contempt for her feelings and disdain for her opinions - that was so very wrong.

The same things apply to my father. I got my personality and optimism from him. He is charming, intelligent and has a wonderful sense of humor. I love his stories and he always has one ready to tell. I love his poetry. I love hearing him singing at the top of his lungs as he tinker on things around the house. Being a consummate Engineer, he is always fixing things for us and is always willing to be there to fix our life mistakes for us as well. He is truly a good father and who has shown great love for each one of his daughters.

Some say that the way you see your own father is the way you see God the Father. I believe that's true. I have had the gift of faith and a reverence for God that came from discussing religion with my dad since I was a little girl. He always told me that the Almighty has looked out for him, his family and that God had his hand on my head. My view of God is shaped by my view of my dad, whom I put on a pedestal growing up. He was loving, thoughtful, caring, exacting in his conditions, and ever-present. Even when my dad traveled a lot for his job, he came back to me bearing a small gift to show me that he was thinking of me. Such a sweet and loving father is a gift from God. This is something I did not understand or realize until I began to pray to have eyes to see and an open heart to understand what it means to honor your father and mother.

My parents were also the ones who taught me the real meaning of servant leadership. Although I had no clue that this was what

Christ had begun in my life a long time ago. When we lived in Pakistan, we had many servants. In fact, our large home had servant's quarters in the back. These were rooms with a connecting bathroom that they could share. There was a bed and their own belongings. The servants could live there so they didn't have to pay to commute (cars were hard to come by for poor people) and basically it was free room and board. Since I grew up with this, I didn't think much of it. It was the norm.

One of the rooms was given to my beloved nanny, Abbai. She didn't stay there, as she was our nanny. She usually slept in our home and in our rooms. She did keep one old-fashioned locked trunk with her few possessions in that little servant's room. The other room was generally occupied by our cook who had to get up early to make meals and stay late to clean up. I never really paid much attention to our cook either, unless I wanted a treat to eat.

The term "Servant" does not have a positive connotation for most people. It means one who is subservient and caters to another's beck and call. My parents did not encourage or discourage us to talk to the house servants - we didn't know them personally, but we were also little girls at the time, so there wasn't much interaction. The only exception was our nanny who was with us continuously and was considered to be an integral part of our family. So she was above the other servants due to her close relationship with the family. I thought of her as my grandmother.

Anyone who has knows about British aristocracy may know that even within the servants, there is a hierarchy. Our "chokeedar" or janitor was probably at the bottom, while my nanny, cook, and inside servants had the higher ranks. I didn't know much about that either, other than seeing my nanny ordering the gardener or chauffeur to do a few things for her. I do recall, however, my mother presiding over the household matters with an air of authority. She was always quiet, never yelling but using her gentle manner in which she carried herself spoke of her rank as lady of the house (usually called "mem sahib" in Urdu). She would gather up the servants and give them their marching orders, especially when we were hosting a party or having guests... which was often.

ALL of this changed, however, when we moved to the United States. My father received multiple job offers that would set our family up for success financially - even more than what we had in Pakistan. When we moved here, it was a rude awakening for all of us, as there were no servants. Not even our beloved Abbai was allowed to come with us (a fact that still brings me to tears as a grown woman due to the love I had for her). We had to make our own meals, do the wash, clean, garden, and do all things that normal American families do - only we weren't normal Americans!

One day, my mother decided to host a party for some of the people we got to know from the Pakistani community. As we set about cooking, early in the morning, we were so excited. It had been a while since we had hosted a party. It took me a little while to realize that the party would not be for us. Instead, we were told not to eat until the guests had eaten (to ensure there was enough hot food on the table) and then to quickly eat so we could do the myriad of dishes by hand, as my mother used her best china for entertaining. We were up until past midnight with the pile of dinner dishes, desert dishes, tea cups, pots and pans from the day's worth of cooking. As my parents had pampered me as their beloved daughter, I was not eager to take on the role of a servant.

The next time there was a party, I was less excited and more wary - was it going to be the same thing again? If so, this was terrible! I began to detest my mother's entertaining because it meant we had to fill in the serving role. We ate last, we worked and yes, we served the guests' every need. This was a sore subject with me even until adulthood. I thought that I would not treat my own children as such (not true anymore, as my husband and I saw what an amazing way this is to raise children - with a servant's heart and attitude)! What an insult to use them as your makeshift servants - or so I thought childishly at that time.

It was not until I met Christ Jesus that I understood why I had been placed in that role. It was a blessing and a gift that my mother gave me. I didn't know that our Lord and Savior came to this earth not to rule with an iron fist, but to serve as a lowly and most humble servant. In John 13, Jesus himself washes the disciples' feet. To take off your clothes, be in your underclothes, is a sign of humility. To wash someone's dirty feet, you have to have them sit or be raised higher than you and then you have to touch those feet with your hands and clean them. This was the job of the lowliest servant in the Eastern home. In Arabia, where there is dust and sand everywhere, there are servants (usually slaves) who wash people's feet. It's disgusting, it's grimy and it's what the Lord of the Lords decided to take upon himself to do for his disciples.

When I read about what Jesus said "But many who are first will be last, and the last first" in both Matthew 19:30 and then again in Matthew 20:16, it made me scratch my head in confusion. It's completely upside down from what the world says about a leader. We should be first in line. We should insist on our rights. No, you shouldn't let someone go ahead of you - you are much more important than that!

Jesus challenged his disciples to think differently. What if you started putting other people first? What would that look like for you? It could be something as simple as allowing someone at the grocery store to go ahead of you. It could be something more difficult like allowing your spouse to have the final say on something you are passionate about. Or at work, it could be to let your employees know that you are there to serve them. Can you imagine what that would do to the home, the workplace and to the world? Maybe people won't notice... at first. I know that for myself, after consistently sending that message with my actions, others began to notice and more importantly, you will begin to notice a change in your own heart.

Even though this is a story of God's grace and redemption, it is a very difficult story to tell. My parents still live in the world of shame and honor. This is a very real and constant value in their community. This chapter addresses my love for my family - a love that is not required merely because they are my parents, but a true love that Christ gives us that overflows into all relationships. It's not easy to love someone who has cut you out of their family not just once but twice. God's love transcends those actions and allows us to heal relationships. It is my hope that if my parents were to read this book, they would understand the true love Christ has given me for them. Not out of honor, obligation or even a social contract. This is a love with no strings attached.

The passage at the start of the chapter comes from 1 Corinthians 13:11-13:"When I was a child, I talked like a child, I thought like a child, I reasoned like a child. When I became a man, I put the ways of childhood behind me. For now we see only a reflection as in a mirror, then we shall see face to face. Now I know in part, then I shall know fully, even as I am fully known. And now these three remain: faith, hope and love. But the greatest of these is love."

When I was a child, I used to speak to my parents in a confused, childish way, think about them with immature thought, and reason about them with my own selfish cares placed first in my mind. But when Christ came into my life, I did away with childish things. Today, I know who I am in Christ and can see what He has done for me. This world can only see His plan dimly, like a reflection in a mirror. The light of heaven removes the confusion of this world and we shall one day see Christ face to face and know his glory. We have assurance of this as His children. I thank God for what He has done in my life in the time that I have been walking with Him. I thank Him for His perfect love through Jesus Christ and the love I now have for my parents. I pray fervently for full restoration with all my family members and that one day they shall have a relationship with Christ.

Chapter 12

The Beginning

There are so many factors that go into changing the entire worldview, customs, culture, belief system for a Muslim. A Muslim who has been transplanted to the United States from an eastern culture is presented with even more issues. The perception of the United States is tainted by what is seen in movies, media and Hollywood. When Muslims turn on the television and see the "Reality TV" shows, they believe that this is how Americans live and what they believe. They readily accept the fact that the United States is a religiously and morally deprived country.

When I teach Cultural Diversity at the college level, my students often laugh at some of the stories I tell about growing up in the East. Things are simply viewed differently on that side of the globe. Time, for example, is looked upon as a completely different entity. Also, the idea of personal space is enormously different in Oklahoma than in New York, much less the eastern hemisphere.

Language varies even more greatly with tone, dialect, accent, etc. One often wonders with all these differences, how do we even get along with one another without stepping all over each other's toes?

I have found that people in the United States are very kind and open to discussions of your background, where you lived, where you grew up and also ethnicity. This is a part of the foundation for the country – Ellis Island was a beacon of hope for many immigrants at the turn of the century. This country is made up of people from all over the world and it is just that type of diversity that brings knowledge and creativity to business.

As I contemplate the differences between the east and the west, I am struck by some of the similarities we all have as human beings: desire to be loved, valued, and treated with respect. Whether I am teaching management or sharing my testimony about Christ, I am almost always asked about my background and point of view on various matters. For some, the idea of a burqa or hijab is of concern: Why do women wear them? Did you have to wear one? Are all women oppressed there? For others, it is the exotic locale of the Middle East or Asia and how everyday life looks like for people there. Yet, there are others who ask me about what my views and thoughts were about Jesus when I was growing up in various Muslim nations.

If you ask a Muslim person about Jesus (by the way, they would LOVE to talk about Jesus – seriously. It is not offensive. Christians just think that Muslims would be offended), you will find that some

Muslims will smile and tell you "We Muslims have more respect for Jesus than you do as Christians." At first, you might not believe this. However, as I mentioned earlier in the book, the Quran has an entire chapter on Christ, titled after his mother, Mary (chapter is called "Maryam"). Mary is the only woman in the Quran to be called by name. She is given a place of high honor and esteem, as Isa is in the Quran. Muslims have to hold all prophets as holy. They believe that the prophets' books are holy. For this reason, Muslims will not say disrespectful things about Jesus because they believe he is a holy prophet of God. This is not always the case in the West. We have the gift of freedom and free speech. It seems like the name of Jesus is a free for all and many people choose to even use his name as a blasphemy (anything that is not held in honor and also using it casually or when you are mad – as a curse word).

The eastern mind operates differently than the western mind. Many times, I am asked "Why" by people. Why does this happen, why would God do this? Why is this the case and why is this written? For those who grew up in eastern countries, the "Why" is not that important, especially when it comes to things of God. If God is sovereign and He wills it, then so be it. Who are you to ask why? There is a huge belief is destiny.

This can be a good and a bad thing. It's good because it places God above mankind and our own understanding. We cannot think through everything and know the answer to everything. We are created beings and God is the supreme Creator. It is a bad thing because the "Why's" are not encouraged. In fact, they are quickly shut down. When I had questions about the Quran or even a lesson in school, it was frowned upon by the elders to keep asking "why? why? why?" This type of thought is regularly discouraged because it is considered a rude challenge to authority. An additional level of complexity to this are the dynamics of men, women and children's roles and places in culture.

So the question is: how does the East come together with the West when we are on absolute opposites points of the compass?

When you look at the Bible, you find some interesting things about people from all over coming to the table of Christ. Luke 13:29 says "And people will come from east and west, and from north and south, and recline at table in the kingdom of God." What does this mean? It means that Christ is preparing a banquet for us. He is getting ready many things in preparation for us to eat with him. How does one do this? He says "Behold, I stand at the door and knock. If anyone hears my voice and opens the door, I will come in to him and eat with him, and he with me" in Revelation 3:20. Christ doesn't mind if you open the door and invite Him to enter, open the door just a crack to stand there and ask questions, or even if you look through the peephole to see who is there. He wants you to know that he is standing there and He invites your questions. He took care to address his disciple Thomas's statements about how he would never believe unless he put his finger into Christ's wounds.

Jesus didn't get furious and say "Thomas, how dare you question if I am the same Christ who was crucified!" Instead, when he later appeared to the whole group, Jesus said "Then he said to Thomas, "Put your finger here, and see my hands; and put out your hand, and place it in my side. Do not disbelieve, but believe" in John 20:27. He is always the sweet Father who lovingly invites His children to bring their questions to Him. He always has the right answers.

Jesus is the only one who can connect the wide gap between the east and the west. The Psalmist wrote "as far as the east is from the west, so far does he remove our transgressions from us" in Psalm 103:12. Those same hands that Thomas wanted to see are the ones that bring the east and the west together through the shedding of blood and redemption in one cross. The picture that comes to my mind is Jesus on the cross, His arms extended with nine inch nails driven through His flesh. Through His sacrifice, He has reconciled East to West, North to South and all ends of the earth. He has bridged the gap horizontally and also vertically by closing the gap between us and God the Father. This is the grace and mercy God shows each one of us. Jesus is the one who provides us the love (enough to die for us), gave us value (allows us to be called children of God), and gives us respect for others (new commandment: love one another as I have loved you), thus meeting the needs no one else can but Christ.

When I became a new Christian, the hope I found in Christ was like nothing I had ever known. For this reason the Bible, speaks often of hope in conjunction with God. There are several verses that talk about the hope we have in Christ. We are called to one body, one Spirit, one Hope (Ephesians 4:4). Faith is also linked to Hope. Faith is confidence in what we hope for and assurance of what we do not see (Hebrews 11:1).

The world is full of hope - over our own strength, financial success and our own might. As a Muslim, I had hope. It was set squarely in my own abilities and in my parents. I believed that my own good works and the good reputation of my family would be enough to carry me along my whole life. Very quickly, that deteriorated. I realized that was a childish attitude and that I had more desire to fulfill my own selfish needs than to help others. I still believed I was a good person, because I didn't understand God's absolute holy nature and that I could not earn my way into His favor. Throwing some change into the red Salvation Army bucket solidified the thought that I was a good person. I chose to place all the hope I had in myself.

As an immigrant, the American Dream played right into my hopes and those of my parents. This is a country like no other. If you try hard enough, you can control your own future, grab your own piece of heaven, and have the freedom to indulge our every desire. As a driven person, I almost burned myself out in the pursuit of an exceptional career. I created competition between my husband and me (my career is better than yours) and I ignored the needs of my children. At the same time, I was quickly making my way up the corporate ladder. I was loved and adored at work.   My hopes and dreams were being fulfilled but there was still an undeniable void. I couldn't figure it out. Maybe if I had more titles, money, prestige, all would be better. I knew nothing of God's promise of rest and peace for the weary and burdened. I knew nothing about His gentleness and promise of rest for our souls (Matthew 11:28). That's what was missing.

It took me several more years until I realized that hope cannot be in myself or in others. When I accepted Christ as my Lord and Savior, there was an immediate sense of relief. God wants you to lay your burdens at His feet and to come to him as you are. You don't have to wait until you are an executive, or until you have met certain goals or achieved a rank or status. In fact, he says "blessed are the meek, for they shall inherit the earth (Matt 5:5)." That is so backwards from what the world says. I think that's why it stays in your brain as a kernel of truth that disrupts thought. These are the things that Muslims here in the United States think about - they don't know that there are answers to the questions they seek to have answered. So many people are fearful based on current events to reach out to Muslims to give them the hope in Christ that is our firm foundation.

Hope belongs to Christ. We cannot lose it because he holds us securely. We can run to him for the hope that shines like a beacon in the dark. Hope beckons us in turbulent times, when the waves of life come crashing down upon us causing us to slip and be tossed about on waves like infants (Ephesians 4:14).

Have you lost hope? Have you looked for it? Have you found it in Christ? Have you confidently approached the throne of God to confess your need for a Savior and to make Him Lord of your life? For the Bible says "We have this hope as an anchor for the soul, firm and secure. It enters the inner sanctuary behind the curtain..." in Hebrews 6:19. I praise Him that I am no longer confined to seeing Allah with my limited knowledge through the Quran, but can see clearly who God the Father is through Christ and the Holy Spirit.

It is difficult to bring my testimony to an end, since God's work is continuous. This chapter is a call to witness and to heed The Great Commission from Matthew 28:16-20 that says "All authority in heaven and on earth has been given to me. Therefore go and make disciples of all nations, baptizing them in the name of the Father and of the Son and of the Holy Spirit, and teaching them to obey everything I have commanded you. And surely I am with you always, to the very end of the age." There is work to be done for God's Kingdom and many people from other countries are here. I moved to the United States when I was ten years old and accepted Christ when I was 35. What a shame that I did not have an authentic witness in my life who shared the pure gospel with me for 25 years. What a joy that even if man will not do it, The Lord still hears those who call upon his name.

The Beginning

May this testimony of what God has done for me bring Him glory. I pray that you will consider these things and see that they point to Christ Jesus. If you invite him into your heart, He will change your vision, your life, your death, and will bring you into eternal life.

Epilogue

It was like a rude awakening from a slow and beautiful dream. The man instantly came out of the house with many rooms and found himself unceremoniously dropped into the middle of an empty dirt road. When he had first been swept away inside the house, the sun was setting and darkness had settled around him. The time it took him to go through the house and speak to the old man in front of the book was like the blink of an eye... yet here he was back outside, looking straight into the rising morning sun. The brilliance of the light caused pain to his eyes because they had adjusted to the darkness. Nothing made sense to him. How was it night one moment and then the brightness of day the next? Who was the man who had grabbed his arm in the street - he never got to see his face, but felt his presence at his side as he guided him through the home. Who was the old man who pronounced the blessing? Why this daughter? Why Mona?

The story from the Prologue was told to me by my father around my tenth birthday. My father had seemed exceptionally thoughtful one morning and I saw him decide suddenly, because he set his teacup down and said "Mona, let's go in the bedroom so I can speak with you privately. I have a story to tell you." When my dad says "I have a story to tell you," I still drop everything because there is nothing else in the world I would rather do than to hear his stories -even those I have heard before. It's a childhood comfort to be near him when he settles in for a long story and shares his gift for storytelling that has been passed down generations.

My dad motioned for me to sit beside him and he began with a serious countenance on his face. He asked me to not share this with my sisters - something he had never done before. He stared off at a distance and told me that he believed God talks to us through dreams and that this vivid dream came to him during Ramadan on the very night I was born. There was something supernatural about it and he wished to tell me so that I would never forget that God truly had His hand on me. He also shared several times in his life where he knew that God was looking out for him in order to emphasize the point that he knew this dream was from God. He said that he was compelled to share with me since it was given to him as the head of the household and that it was a sign that I was set apart for His purpose.

Dreams carry a spiritual significance for Muslims, and this takes on extra importance during Laylat al Qadr. For as I mentioned in the first chapter, I was born during Ramadan which is the holiest month of the year, on Laylat al Qadr – the night of destiny or the night of power. It is the holiest night of Ramadan. Muslims believe that it's the only night God opens up the channels between heaven and earth and allows mankind to speak directly to Him. In addition, many Muslims pray specifically for His guidance through dreams.

At that time, I had no clue what that purpose might be. As a child, all you know is that when your father is speaking to you in hushed terms of awe, there is something significant about it and that it should never be disregarded. Now, after knowing what Christ has done for me, I know that the Bible says we are chosen and we are set apart for His purpose.

The Lord chose to reveal His truth to my dad many years ago in that specific way that has great importance for the eastern world. This is consistent with the Scriptures, as The Lord spoke to many through dreams and He continues to do so with those He calls. The events in the dream are applicable to all who belong to Christ, not just to me. We have a heavenly Father who loves us and has reached down from Heaven to tell us that His hand is upon us. When God places His hand upon us, He strengthens us for all good work. In the Bible, 1 Peter 2:9 sums up my father's dream by saying "But you are a chosen people, a royal priesthood, a holy nation, God's special possession, that you may declare the praises of him who called you out of darkness into his wonderful light." May this be a reminder for all those who belong to Christ Jesus.

About the Author

Mona Sabah Earnest was born and raised in the Middle East (Saudi Arabia, Kuwait and United Arab Emirates), England, went to school in Pakistan and then finally moved to the United States. She speaks English, Spanish, and Urdu fluently. She has worked in the Human Resources field and teaches Management, Leadership and Cultural Diversity. She holds her Masters in Human Resources from the University of San Francisco. She is a professional speaker and a corporate trainer.

Mona became a follower of Jesus Christ at the age of 35. She has been married to Stephen since 1993 and has three beautiful children. Her mission statement is: To be a light for the Kingdom of God by sharing my testimony of faith in my Lord & Savior Jesus Christ and by equipping the Church to be an authentic witness to share the Gospel.

BLOG: https://monaearnest.wordpress.com/
PUBLISHER BLOG: https://fromisatochrist.wordpress.com/
AUTHOR PAGE: https://www.facebook.com/Mona-Sabah-Earnest/

Appendix

Frequently Used Terms with Pronunciation:

Allah [Ul-Lah]- Arabic name for God, meaning one God

Allahuakbar [Ul-lahu-Ak-Baar]- Arabic saying "God is great" (called the Takbir)

Apostate - One who renounces a religious belief

Burqa [Boor-Kah]- A woman's outer garment that covers her (same as Niqab [Nee-Cob])

Five Pillars of Faith:

1. Shahadah: reciting the Muslim profession of faith.
2. Salat: ritual prayers in the proper way five times daily.
3. Zakat: paying an alms (or charity) for poor and the needy.
4. Sawm: fasting during the month of Ramadan.
5. Hajj: pilgrimage to Mecca.

Hijab [Hee-Job]- Means to cover (usually face, hair, neck, upper body)

Hadith [Haw-Deeth]- Traditions of prophet Mohammad

Imam [Ee-Mom]- Muslim leader, holy person, or cleric

Injeel [Een-Jeel]- Arabic name of the Gospels given by Allah to Isa

Isa [Ee-Saw]- Arabic name for Jesus in the Quran

Isa Ibn Maryam - Jesus, son of Mary

Islam [Ee-Slaam]- Arabic word for submission or surrender

Kafir [Kaw-Fir] - Worst name given to an unbeliever and an apostate

Laylat al Qadr - Arabic for night of destiny or night of power

Mehndi [Men-Dee]- Ceremony surrounding a paste made from the henna plant

Mohammad or Muhammad (same) - Prophet & founder of Islam. (A.D. 570-A.D. 632)

Mosque [Moss-k]- Place of prayer (also called Masjid [Mass-jed])

Muslim[Moose-slim] - Arabic for "one who submits"

Quran [Koor-Ahn]- Muslim holy book (also called "Koran"). Arabic word that means "to recite"

Ramadan: Annual period of 30 days of fasting for Muslims

Surah [Soo-Rah]- Arabic word for a Chapter in the Quran

Ummah [Uma]- Global community of Muslims

Made in the USA
Columbia, SC
07 July 2019